Life after the Storm

A Memoir

Mrs. J

Life After the Storm

Copyright © Janice Roberts (Mrs. J) 2018

Truth Seeker Publishing
7611 South Broadway
St Louis, Mo 63111

www.truthseekerspublishing.com   email: truthseekers.publishing@yahoo.clm

Quantity sales. Special discounts are available on quantity purchases by corporations, associations, and others. For details, contact the publisher at the address above.

Orders by U.S. trade bookstores and wholesalers.

ISBN-13:
978-1987794236

ISBN-10:
1987794230

Printed in the United States of America

Truth Seeker Publishing

DEDICATION

This is for my Daughter, Carita. Thank you for being the most loving and caring daughter any mother could ask for. We have traveled down many rough roads together, God carried us through.

Thank you for helping me through difficult times and loving me unconditionally. I am so blessed to have you as a part of my life. You are my daughter and best friend. You have bought out the best in me. I now know that I can overcome anything.

Love Mom

Mrs. J

ACKNOWLEDGMENTS

I would like to thank my Mom and Dad for giving me life. I send out my very appreciation to my grandma and grandpa for giving me a home to stay and being the best parents that they could possibly be. I thank my grandparents for being instrumental in my Christian walk by taking me to church on Sunday.

Special thanks to my grandpa for all his love and being a father to me until his death. Thank you to my child hood friends who always answers when I call. Thank you to my Christian friends that I met while living in Izmir, Turkey. Thank you for your prayers and leading me to Christ.

Also, a very special thank you to a special minister for telling me there is life after the storm.

It was an extraordinary fall day on November 7. I was born. My mom and Dad have a total of 4 children, a total of three girls and one boy. I was the youngest of them all. My mother divorced my father when she was three months pregnant with me. After the divorce, she went about her life. She was not around much when I was younger. When I was one year old, my mother remarried and moved out of the state with her husband. She left us with our grandparents. She promised after she got things in order she would come back to get us. When she got there, she found out her husband was already married. Her so-called mother in law told her that was not the first time he married someone and brought her to meet her. She said he was already married and had A WIFE, and they were expecting a baby. My mom was so heartbroken and ashamed. She called her mother and began to cry about the news she had found out; her mother told her to come home her four kids needed her. Two months had passed, my mother didn't return. After six months her mother begged her to come home. She still didn't listen. After nine months of being away from her four small children, her father talked to her on the phone and told her to come back home to her family. She became very sick while she was out of town. At the end of 9 months she called and asked for someone to come get her. My grandmother called her brother and asked him to get his niece. He lived out of town. He left to go and get my mom her parents was so worried about her they had not seen her in almost a year. They were so glad she decided to come home when she returned I was told she could hardly walk all of her hair had fallen out she never would tell anyone what had happened to her.

While she was living out of town, there were rumors that my mother wouldn't come back home because she had gotten pregnant while there. It was also said that she had a baby. That is why mom was gone for nine months. Since she knew she was not legally married, she was ashamed. More rumors were told that the baby was left with her husband's mother. I asked my mother do I have another brother or sister; she denied it. She denied it and said it was not true and it was a lie that was made up by my grandmother's neighbors across the street. I still wonder to this day do I have a brother or sister out there somewhere.

I remember when I was three years old, I can remember my grandfather would keep his lighter fluid for his gun on a sherro (wardrobe). That is what they called it back then. Today it would be called a cabinet. I saw something that stood out to me. I noticed something very bright and red. I was curious. I pulled a chair across the room and climbed to reach the bright red shiny container. I stretched my arms and fingers until I reached it. Yepee! I got it I got down and opened the little red top that was on it and began to drink. Whatever it was tasted horrible. I put it back on the sherro. When I climbed down, my grandmother came in the room. She asked me, "what is that smell?" I said I drank that shiny red thing on the sherro. My grandmother ran over and got that lighter fluid to see how much I drank. I had drunk half the can. I began to feel dizzy and nauseated. My grandmother ran to the kitchen and got some grease that she had cooked some meat with. She had it laying on top of the stove. She gave me a half a cup and told me to drink it the next thing I knew I was unconscious my grandmother laid me down on the bed I stayed that way for over 12 hours. When I finally woke up I could not remember what had happened. If it was not for my grandmother's home remedies, they didn't take you to the doctor. I could've died drinking that poison. Thanks to God who was right there with me. Maybe, I should have gone to the doctor.

I remember when I was four years old, my grandparents would go to Offutt, Mississippi to visit their relatives. They would leave us with my uncle's girlfriend. I don't remember where my mother was at that time; I remember my grandparents would leave us on a Sunday. While they visited their family, my siblings and I would play outside with the ladies kids. We would eat the lunch my grandmother would pack for us. I didn't understand why we had to share our lunch with my uncles' girlfriend's children.

My siblings and I stayed with our grandparents. They were very nice to us. I love my grandfather so much. He would bring us snacks from the store. We would wait up for him to come home at night just for that goody bag. That bag would be loaded with ice-cream, potato chips, candy, cookies, and soda pop. YUM YUM! My uncle would also wait up with us for the snacks my grandpa bought. My uncle would wait up so he could take some of my oldest sister snacks. She got tired of him. One day, my grandpa had brought us an ice-cream sandwich. She licked all around it so he would not take it from her. He was so angry, but he never did hit her because my grandpa would not have allowed it.

Christmas time was very fun at my grandparents' house. I would wonder where my mother was. We did not see her very often. She wasn't around in our life during the Christmas holidays

I could smell the chicken and dressing, sweet potato pie, and greens cooking. My grandparents' house was very old. My grandparents had a gas heater that sat on the floor. One cold winter when I was five year old I was so cold that I was standing in front of the heater. I just could not get warm. I kept backing back closer to the heater until I got too close and burned the back of my leg. Ouch!!!!! It was a very bad burn. I had a very big blister on the back of my leg. One day I was skating in the house I fell and burst my blister. It hurt really bad, to this day I still have that scar on the back of my leg.

When I was about seven years old my grandmother's brothers came down from Mississippi to visit. I think that would have made them my great uncles. She had cooked a big dinner for them .I was so hungry, I asked my grandma if I could eat. She told me no, let my brothers eat first then you can eat. I was starving. she told me I had to wait but had not eaten anything that day.   I was felt so bad I wanted to eat. I heard all her brothers in the kitchen eating and laughing so I went around the side of the house at the kitchen window. I peep in there and saw how they was eating and talking they took such a long time eating. So I pick up something and threw it at the window and took off running OMG!!!   The window broke. I was so scared I ran and hid. I didn't mean to break the window, I did not know it was going to break   I was trying to get their attention. My great uncles came out of that out kitchen running out the door. They found me and asked me why I did that. I said I wanted to eat like you all were eating. My grandmother said you better not do that again with your bad self. Since that day I always thought I was a bad girl. My grandmother used to tell me that the devil was going to stick a pitch fork in my back. When I go to sleep, and take me to hell if I didn't act right. Maybe sometimes I was hard headed. I would be scared to sleep on my stomach at night. I was scared the devil was going to get me. I would never sleep on my stomach, even after I had grown up. I still remember what my grandmother told about that pitchfork. I was never a bad girl. I just did typical things a little girl would do.

My grandpa used to cut grass.   I used to ride with him in his truck. He had a light blue Ford pickup truck. It was so fun to watch him cut the grass.   I played on the sidewalk until after he finished. He loaded up his riding lawn movers on the back of his truck. We would stop by a store on our way home. He always bought me ice cream. YAY!   I was happy. I loved my grandpa.

I was never with my father growing up. He would come by to visit now and then. He was an alcoholic. My grandmother would tell me stories about how he would treat my mother, sisters, and brother. She told me how he would come home drunk. Once my mother was watching TV, he kicked the TV. He took his foot and kicked the screen out and broke it.

One of the neighbors, a lady that lived down the street would call her and warn her that she saw my dad coming. My dad would pick sticks to hit my mother with. My mom knew that the stick he picked up he was going to use it on her. My mom would grab my sister and brother and run under the house for safety she would hold her hand over their mouth so he did not hear them breathing. I wasn't born during that time. My grandmother said my mom was scared and she knew he would not find her under the house. He was an abusive father. When my middle sister was about five months old, my dad would hold her and let her fall to the floor. He did both my sisters and brother that way. My grandmother said she was so glad that I did not have to go through that. She told me how he would not provide for his family. Many times they did not have food or milk to drink. The utilities were always disconnected. The furniture was purchased on credit; when it wasn't paid for it was repossessed.

He would always come home drunk and beat on my mother. She had just had my oldest sister. She was only a few days old; my mom was in bed from having the baby. He came in the house drunk: pulled my mom by the ankles and threw her on the floor. Another time my mom was trying to go to work; my dad came to the bus stop and beat her up for no reason. He struck her in the face so hard that she saw stars. It was such a hard hit and gave her a black eye. He beat her all the way back home. After my mother divorced my dad; she just went about her life without her children. We didn't live with her. We all lived with our grandparents because that's where she left us. My grandparents were gracious enough to take all four of us.

I would ride my bike and would see my dad coming down the street. I never will forget how his leg was crossing over one another. OMG!!!!!! He was calling my name as loud as he could over and over again. I was so scared: I start paddling my bike as fast as I could. It seemed like I was not going anywhere. Maybe because I was so afraid to see him walking like that I never saw anything like that before. He looked like a monster to me. I thought he was going to get me. I rode my bike as fast as I could to my grandparents' house. I told her what had happened I looked out the window to see if I saw him coming down the street but he went another way. I was so glad what a relief.

My brother was not very nice. He would fight his sisters. He was older than me. One day he tried to take something I was eating. I didn't let him have it. He hit me as hard as he could on my forehead. He struck me, and I got a large lump. Luckily, it went back down, and no one found out what he did to me. I did not tell my grandparents. He was a very mean brother. He was always taking our things. One day he got so mad at me I ran and hid in my grandparent's closet. He tried his best to get me, but my grandma made him leave me alone. I was not very close to him. He was so different from all of us.

My grandpa was nice to me. I use to sit in his lap on the porch. He would take me with him to the peach patch. I remember I had a shirt on with my back out and a pair of shorts on the peaches was so sticky and hairy I start to itch badly. I wanted to leave and go home. When we finally left, I was miserable. While I was riding back home in the truck all, I could think of when I get home was taking a cold bath. It was so hot out; I never wanted to go back again.

One Sunday before church my grandfather broke off a switch from the tree because I didn't want to listen. That morning he gave me a whooping. I guess I was hard headed I can't remember what I did but I had on stockings with my dress, and the switch tore my stockings I couldn't wear them to church. I cried and cried my grandmother told him that he should not have done that I had welts all over my legs. I was so sad that Sunday morning.

I found out my mother remarried when I was 9 years old. I have a stepfather. He was not a mean stepdad, but he was much older than my mom. My siblings and I continued to live with my grandparents. My mother had a job working at the factory. On Friday nights she would pick us up for the evening this made me so happy because I never stayed with her. She would cook us hamburger helper. We would watch TV and enjoy our time with her. After we watched TV, we went to bed. We always had to leave at 10 am the following morning. My mom said we had to leave so that my grandmother could get us ready for church on Sunday. I really wished we could have stayed the weekend with our mom. When we got back to our grandparent's house she would wash our hair in some kind of silver wide pan. She would wash our hair with dial soap. We didn't have any shampoo and pressed our hair with a straightening comb that she would put on the stove to get hot. We didn't have a blow dryer. While our hair was still wet, I could hear the sizzling as the straightening comb went down my hair. I wish my mom could have been around us more than she did I only saw her on the weekend for a short period I always wondered why.

It was Christmas Eve at my grandparents' house again. I think I was ten years old now. I remember my grandparents said I wasn't going to get any toys for Christmas because I had been so bad. I wonder what I did. Maybe it was a habit of them saying that to me. I went to bed early about 7:00 P.M hoping Santa would sneak me in some toys. I woke up about midnight. I heard something, and I got up out of bed very quietly and went to the living room. I peeped through a hole that was in the door I thought I saw Santa clause putting toys out I ran back to bed pull the covers over my head shut my eyes tight so Santa would not put ashes in my eyes and went back to sleep the next morning I woke up I ran to the living room and found our toys Santa left me some toys I was so happy. We had two couches in the living room. Everybody had a little section where their toys were. Santa always left us a shoebox full of apples, oranges, nuts, and candy. I wish my mother could of have spent Christmas with us. I don't if she even called that day.

At my grandparents' house, we only had three bedrooms. My grandpa and grandma had a room. I used to sleep in the middle between them since I was the youngest. My two sisters had the middle room, and my bother slept in the back room. Sometimes my uncle will sleep in the back room with my brother when he was over. It was a bed and a fold up bed. As I got older, I started to sleep in the middle room with my sister. I was in the middle again I would pee in the bed sometimes. It used to make my sisters very mad at me. We would all had to get up, and my grandmother would scrub the mattress and put some plastic on top of it. She would get some clean sheets, and we returned to sleep. My oldest sister decided she did not want to sleep with us anymore. I guess she was getting older; she probably was about thirteen. I remember her asking my grandmother could she sleep in the living room. She told her she could. She made that her room. I had to sleep next to the wall. I was so scared there were bugs crawling on the wall. I saw a praying Mathis on the wall one night. Boy was I scared. I called my grandpa to kill it. I could hear rats and mice in the garbage can in our room. At night I pulled the covers over my head. I was so scared bugs would get in my ears while I was in the bed. It was terrifying going to sleep at night. I would always look behind the bed and all around the room before I went to bed. I still do that till this day.

I have two uncles. My youngest uncle lived with us sometimes. Most times he resided with his girlfriend. He would drink all the time. My grandmother said he was an alcoholic. His girlfriend sometimes would come over to the house to pick him up. She had a mother that keep a towel over her face. I didn't know why or understood why she would walk around with a bath towel over her head and cover her face. My youngest uncle said one night when he was over his girlfriend house; he said he was drunk and he went in her mother room by mistake and pulled that towel off of her head, and he couldn't believe what he saw under that towel. So many holes in her face he said he could see her teeth through some of those holes. He said she looked really bad.

I remember my uncle and grandfather arguing a lot because he was drunk at the house. He would come home drunk in a cab, and someone would help him get out the cab because he was too drunk to walk. He did not have the money to pay the taxi, so my grandmother would pay the fee. I still remember the name of the cab. It was Jolly Cab Company. One night, my uncle came home with welts all over his body. My grandfather, which is his father, he asked him what happened. He said he was whip with a tire tube. I didn't see it, but I remember my grandparents talking about it. He was working for a service station called the Brown Boys. My grandfather went to their service station to find out why they did that to his son. He found out that my uncle was trying to fight them because he was drunk and they beat him up. My grandfather was very upset about what happened, but he did start that fight, and he met his match.

When I was 12 years old, my grandfather had a stroke. He used to cut grass. One day he got too hot and suffered a heat stroke. The temperature that day was sweltering. My grandfather was in his late 60's when that happened. I was so glad he was ok. I loved my grandpa. He loved to cut grass and do yard work. He was ok for about a year. He continued to cut grass in the summer. He had another stroke, it was on Labor Day in September. I remember him talking funny, and a big vein in his arm was jumping. My grandmother said Son that is what she called him, do you want me to call the ambulance? He said No I am ok. His speech started sounding very funny very thick-tongued. He went to the bathroom and staggered back to the front room about 30 mins later. He said somebody call the ambulance. I knew something had to be wrong because he hated going to the doctor. I was terrified. My grandmother called my mother and told her what happened. My mom said when he got to the hospital he had had 7s strokes one after another. He was admitted to intensive care. He was paralyzed from head to toe. The only thing he could move was his eyes. I remember going to see him at the hospital. When I saw him, I would say, grandpa, if you can hear me move your eyes. He started rolling his eyes fast. I wanted him to get better so he could come home again. I would call the hospital every night and ask how my grandpa is doing. The nurse would say he is still critical condition. On the second week of being in the hospital, I called the hospital checking on my grandpa. The nurse asked me what relationship I have with him. I said I was his granddaughter. She said he had passed away a few mins ago. I remember crying. I love my grandpa, he was like my father. I ran and told my grand mom what the nurse said. She was quiet. She didn't show any emotion. My uncles and my mother was at the hospital when he died. The nurse had called my mom to the hospital because they knew he was dying. My mom said when she got to the hospital she ran as fast as she could down the hallway trying to see him one last time. my mom was so angry with me for telling my grand mom the news that grandpa had died. She said she wanted to tell her. I loved him too. my uncle told my grandmother that my   grandfather raised up with both hands stretch out like he was making a v. He said dad is getting better and then he lowered himself back to the bed and died. My grandpa was free. I know my mother promised him that she would take of us.

I will never forget my grandfather's funeral. I still remember as I am writing now. There were two family cars. There were lots of flowers. That was a sad day for me.   I just could not stop crying. As I was sitting there on the second row in the church, someone sang a song, Hold on to God's Unchanging Hand. That song had me feeling sad looking at him lying in that casket. It was a gray casket. I remember tears just rolling down my face. I looked at my grandmother. She was trying to be strong, but she just couldn't hold it any longer. She started to cry, but she could not keep the tears back. The funeral director rolled the casket in front of the place where my grandmother other relatives were sitting. It just made it worst my grandfather sister had to be carried out of the funeral. Two men carried her out like she was sitting in a chair. Later I found out the reason for that was because she had poop on herself. He had

.e sisters. After the funeral was over, we headed to the cemetery.
. looked back while sitting in the family car. I was in the second car.
I saw so many cars following the hearse to the graveyard. It seemed
to me like it was about 100 cars. My grandfather was well liked
around the town; I guess since he cut so many people grass. After my
grandfather had died, I would sleep in the bed with my grandmother.
I slept on his side of the bed. I could still smell his scent on his
pillow. I always wondered if that was his spirit comforting me. I
missed my grandpa so much I never forgot my memories. I had with
him he was a special grandpa to me.

My youngest uncle was staying with his girlfriend for a while, but
after my grandfather died he decided to come back and live with my
grandmother. He said he didn't want his mother to be alone. My
uncle would come home drunk all the time like he used to. When he
did stay there sometimes, he would say bad words to my
grandmother. Sometimes he and my brother would fist fight. They
would fight in the middle of the floor. My uncle was drunk and my
grandmother would call my mom. She would came over to try to
stop the fight. My uncle was very abusive to my sisters and me. He
called us bitches.   I remember when my grandmother would tell us
don't say anything be quite so he won't get worse. I did not
understand why we had to be called names like that. Those names
made me feel bad about myself.

When we wanted to use the telephone to call our friends: we
would have to ask our uncle. He would ask how long we were going

to be on the phone. I didn't understand it was my grandparents' house. I wish my mom could have taken us away with her: being there was awful!!!!

I used to love when the newspaper come. I like reading my horoscope and Dear Abby. I would be waiting on the porch. When I saw the newspaper boy, I ran outside to meet him. My uncle took the newspaper from me and said for me not to mess with that paper until he read it. It was my grandmother's newspaper. She   paid all the bills in her house. He just stayed there and ruled everything. My grandmother was too scared to say anything to him about the way he treated everybody. I hated living in that house. I really wish my grandpa was still alive. I wanted to go live with my mom, but she had her own life with her husband.   When my grandpa died, I felt like all my protection was gone. I was all alone. My grandma was not the same as my grandpa. I would be sitting down in a chair, and my uncle would walk past me and say you, stupid bitch. I got so mad at him. I got fed up and yelled stop calling me those names. He came after me I ran out the house into the streets, and he was running behind me. I was scared. I almost fell going down the steps. I was scared he was going to hurt me.   I tried to get away. I was afraid he was going to catch me.   I ran as fast as I could so he couldn't catch me. He never did. I was so scared if he did what would he could had done to me.

My grandma saw what was happening and didn't say or do anything. I thank God I got away that time. Sometimes I would go in the living room, and he would come in there. Starting up something with me fussing. He was drunk; I was sitting on the couch and all of a sudden he grabbed me by the neck and started choking me. My grandmother heard a noise. She came in the living room and found her grown son choking me with both hands. She tried to pull him off of me. My eyes were rolling back in my head. Somehow she pulled him off of me. I got away. He could have killed me that day. No one called the police. My grandmother told me just to be quiet and don't say anything when he says things to you so he can leave you alone. That is all I ever heard to be quiet and let him do what he wants. I wanted him dead! I hated him! My neck was bruised. I hated my life! I wish I could go with my grandpa. My uncle was a terrible person. My mom only wanted to live her life without us with her husband. I wanted someone who could love me.

One Sunday we went to church, and my uncle stayed home. My mother drove all of us to church and took us back home. When we got back to my grandmother's house, my uncle was sitting in my grandmother chair with her shotgun pointed toward the door. When we came in the door, my grandmother rushed over to him and grabbed the gun and wrestled him to the floor. She managed to get the gun from him. He was also drunk on that day. It was like he was going to shoot all of us. Luckily, the weapon did not go off, and we weren't killed.

One day someone from the next street called my grandmother and told her that my uncle was stone drunk and had passed out on the road. So she asked my middle sister, she was 15 teen at the time,

16

to help her go and get my uncle. I remember looking out the window and seeing them dragging my uncle back to the house on the front porch. He was still passed out. They had him by his arms: his legs were dragging on the ground. They pulled him through the house knocking over a chair and other stuff. My sister was so tired of dragging that massive grown man. She saw some of her friends, and she said they were laughing at her. She said that was the most embarrassing moment in her life. I could see the look on her face. They put him on the bed in the back room. As soon as they laid him down, he awakened and started fussing. He was fussing and telling all of us that there were naked women outside in my grandmother flower bed. My grandmother loved flowers; she had a green thumb for flowers. He was so drunk he could not even walk. So he crawled out the house into the yard trying to find those naked women. He was crawling, and he was messing up my grandmother flowers. I was frightened and started to cry. There was no one there to comfort me. It was like I was all by myself. If only my mom have been an active mother. My life would have been so much different.

I am sweet sixteen now. I called myself liking a boy. I believe he liked me too. I can't remember his name, but I was excited. We would talk on the telephone when my uncle was not around. He sure did guard that telephone. If I were on the phone, he would say if I didn't get off that phone he would tear it out the wall. He had a hold to the cord sitting on the floor ready to pull it out of the wall. He even yanked on it, but again my grandmother would tell me don't say anything for peace. She always told me to do what he said. I wanted my grandmother to put him out of the house. I hated him. He made my life so bad for no reason. We could not go stay with our mother. She did not want us there. She knew how abusive her brother was, but never did anything about it. Why did she not do anything about it? Why did I have to continue living like that? I wanted to run away. I missed my grandpa. I wish he would come back and save me.

My uncle had an accident. He had to have one of his legs amputated. He had gain green in his leg. He never let it heal the right way. He was always drunk, falling over and hurting his leg. The doctors had to take his leg. He was in the hospital for about 2 months and that was the best time I have had since my grandpa had died. I did not want him to come back ever again. My sisters and brothers didn't want him back either. We were not terrified we felt free and safe.

When my uncle got well, he returned home. That was a very sad day for the rest of my siblings and me. We wanted him to never to come back there again. As time went by, he continued to get drunk. He only had one leg, and the other was cut off above the knee. He would use his crutches and throw it at us when he was drunk. We had to run and dodge those crutches so it would not hit us in our head. He was so mean. I wonder what caused him to be mean to us. He was way older than us. We were just teenagers. It was horrible being harassed and abused by a grown man. My uncle was a bully.

We had nowhere to go; so we had to stay there and take it. One night I would not get off the telephone. Nobody needed to use it. I was on the phone for about 5 minutes. He said get off that phone. I did not get off, so he got so mad and told me he did not want me on it. So when I didn't get off, he hopped himself in the room where I was and sat on the floor in an Indian style. He grabbed the telephone cord and said if you don't get off the telephone I will yank it out the wall. I mean get your ass off now!!!!!! I asked him why I need to get off. I said it loud so he could hear me. He told me I would get you when you go to sleep. I was so nervous and scared I stayed up all night because I didn't want him to hurt me while I was sleep. I thought he was going to kill me. I didn't get any sleep that night. I was sleepy. I wanted a new home. I whispered to myself and said grandpa, please come back to me. I miss you so much. My grandpa wouldn't have allowed my uncle to do those terrible things to us. He would have put him out that house. He would have taken good care of me. I felt like I was a horrible person. My grandma would talk to my mother on the phone. They would discuss how mischievous I was. What did I do? Maybe because sometimes I talked back to my uncle. I was so tired of him. I was getting fed up with his treatment.

The next time I saw my mother was when she came over to my grandmother house to bring my uncle some beer on a Friday evening. She told me to be quiet so he would not hit me. She knew she did not want to be bothered with it. So if we would be quiet, she did not have to come over that often. I believe they thought if you would not say anything and let him say what he wanted he would leave you alone. All I heard is be quiet and don't say anything. In other words, they were teaching me to take whatever he does to me.

I was not very smart in school. I didn't try like I should have in school since my parents would tell me that I was dumb. The reason they said that is because my grades were terrible. They never encouraged me or even tried to help me with school. They never wanted to push me in doing my school work. When I made terrible grades, they just put me down. Maybe that is another reason they considered me to be a bad girl. I love to dress up for school. I liked to look nice. I always took care of my appearance. Since my mom did not stay with us, she never did show any concerns about my grades either. When I took my report card home to get it signed by a parent. I would call my mom on the phone to let her know about the grades that I made. She didn't show any concern. She didn't tell me to study or offer me any tutoring. She never saw not even one of my report cards she was too busy living her own life and not being in her children's life. She would tell me to tell my sister to sign her name on my report card. I thought that was so bad. Looking back, I wasn't dumb. I didn't have anybody to be concerned about me or encourage me or tell me school was necessary. No one showed any love.

I remember sitting on my grandmother front porch every day waiting for my mother to drive by on her way home from work. I wanted to see her. When she would pass by, I would get excited. When I saw her car getting closer to the house, I stood up waving at her she would blow her horn and keep driving. I wish she could have stopped and said hello to me and give me a hug. I would wait for her every day.

I was raised up in a dysfunctional home with an abusive uncle and being scared all the time. I had a grandmother that wanted you to take abuse from my uncle for peace. A mother that didn't any responsibilities. My grandmother never told me good things about myself. My grandmother and mother would support my uncle bad habits. My grandmother would send my mom to the store to buy beer. He drank Colt 45. My grandmother did not want the neighbors to see them bringing beer in the house, so my mom would back her car in the driveway and take the beer in the backdoor. She would buy cases at a time. They were so worried about the neighbors. I thought to myself why they are buying him all that beer.

If I wanted any of my friends to come to visit me, my grandmother would ask my uncle would it be ok. Sometimes he would say yes, and sometimes he would say no. If he said no they would tell him they would give him a beer and if he said yes. He would set the time for my friends to leave and if they didn't, he would come in that living room and run everybody out of the house. My uncle controlled everybody. He ruled that house. He was so mean. I hated him. I didn't understand.

One night my uncle was so drunk and terrorizing the house. He was starting trouble for no reason. He came over toward me while I was sitting in my grandmother room and said stop rocking that chair.

Since I didn't stop rocking in the chair, he grabbed me and tore my shirt off of me and took his fingernails and scratched up my back so bad. It looked horrible. My back was bleeding. My grandmother and sisters tried to stop him, but he knocked both of them down. My grandmother got up that is when he took his fist and hit her in the eye. She had a black eye. My sister called the police. When the cops got there, they looked at my back and said we could get him for child abuse. They saw my grandmother eye. They took my uncle and threw him in the police car without his crutches. He went to jail that night, but he got out the next day. My grandmother said it was wrong that the police did not let him have his crutches. It was like they felt sorry for him. How could they after what he did to us? No one pressed any charges against him. He was back home again the next morning. I hated him!

I met this guy while at school. I thought he was cute. He asked me to be his girlfriend. I liked him. He would come and visit me sometimes if my uncle said he could. . We dated for less than a year. I would see him at the basketball game. He would come over to the house and sit with me. I was so happy being with him. One night my high school had a party. I met him there. We had t-shirts made. We wore them to the party for some reason he got mad at me and took his shirt off. His shirt had my name on it and vice versa. , so he took his off and gave it back to me. My feelings were hurt and I wanted to leave the party. It was a girl there, and she saw what happened. She said to me why you feel bad. I didn't want to be there anymore. So I left. During that time you could walk home alone. Times wasn't bad as is now. She walked with me.   I started crying. She said,   why are you crying? I told her because he gave me back my shirt and he was so mad at me. She told me that I should not whine about something like that. She said forget him, but I didn't.   I dated him for about another month. Finally, I got tired of the lies he was telling me. I found out he was cheating on me.   I also found out that he drinks alcohol. I didn't want anybody that bad, so I finally cut him loose. I wish my mom could have been there for me.   I feel like my life would have been different. I wanted someone to care about me so bad.   I made wrong choices, but God was always with me.

Some rumors was told around school that my ex-boyfriend was beating me up. He never lifted a hand to hit me. The girl that I met at the party became my best friend.

At the age of sixteen, I would see the newspaper boy doing his route. I would be sitting on my grandmother's porch. He always stared at me but never said anything. I wasn't interested in him. The school was out for the summer. When school started back, in the fall, I would be going to high school. I was so excited about high school. I thought high school was something big. Finally, summer is over. Time for school and I was happy. My first day I remember I was so nervous.   I was in the tenth grade I met some new friends.   I took cosmetology. I loved doing hair. My teacher was lazy. She hardly taught us anything. I remember her showing us how to use a curling iron. Let's see what else she taught us, maybe how to shampoo our hair and do a roller set. We played a lot. She just sat there doing nothing. Rumors were she came to school drunk. Something was wrong for her just to sit there like that. We should have reported her, but I guess we were young and did not know any better. I didn't care a lot about a school. I just made sure I looked nice each day and wore cute clothes. There was a lot of girls that was jealous of me. They talked about me with words like she thinks she is so cute. I had a lot of haters while in high school. One day my telephone rang while I was at home. Some girl said on the other end said you think you are so cute she would call me every morning before school and after school. I never knew who she was or recognize her voice. She called me every day for a long time. I think that entire year.

I saw this guy and he look so familiar. He went to the same school I went to. I remember he was the newspaper guy who threw the newspaper on the street of my grandmother house. He was kind of popular. A lot of girls liked him. I thought he was ugly, but for some reason, I wanted to talk to him. So I would get in his view at school. One day he noticed me and started to talk to me. I was smiling, but I was not attracted to him. I spoke to him because other girls did. I did not have a boyfriend at the time, so I talk to him off and on. One day I saw him at the school walking down the hall. I called his name to get his attention. He waited for me to come down the steps. We started dating after that. He would come over my grandma house to see me; my uncle was there as well ,drunk. My mother would have to give him beer so I could have my boyfriend to come and visit me. He was so mean when he was ready for him to leave he would hop himself right in there and tell my boyfriend to get out his house. I got so tired of how he treated me. I called my mom and asked her could I stay with her. She said I could, I was shocked

My mother was not very kind to me. She thought I was having sex with my boyfriend, but I was not. She would tell me things like my vagina probably was bigger than hers. That really did hurt my feelings. I didn't understand how that could be. I was not having sex and I haven't had any children. That made me cry. I felt like I left my grandma house but I still was not happy. She never complimented me. When we went to church on Sunday she would come back home bragging about how pretty this other girl was at the church we attended. She was a beautiful girl. She always boast on other people. She never told me she loves me or hugged me. One day we were having a conversation about my biological father. She told me she wished she had only had one child by him. She only wanted my oldest sister. I thought to myself Wow!!!!!

When I was 17, I continued to date my boyfriend. He would call me on the telephone at my mother house. He had a birthday coming so I baked him a cake. I was so excited my mother took me over to his house in her car so I could give him his birthday cake. That night when he called me on the telephone he made fun of the cake I baked for him. He said it was burned and his mother had to cut the bottom out of it. That made me feel so sad. I really tried to do something special on his birthday. When I got off the phone I started crying. I never made him another cake again.

My mother would drop me off at my grandmother house on her way to work so I could walk to school. The school was not that far from my grandmother house. One day my mother started being nicer to me. She bought me a car. I was so surprised. I told her thanks. I was so glad I didn't have to walk to and from school anymore. I showed my boyfriend my new car. It wasn't a brand new car but it was ok for me. Again he made fun of my car. He said it was not a good car and my mother needed to take it back. That really made me mad. He thought he knew everything and thought he was so smart. Maybe since his stepdad was a mechanic. His stepdad had a gas station and taught him things about cars. He would go down after school to help him. I did feel bad because everything I tried to do he would put me down. I thought he would have said something nice. I would pick him up almost every day after he would work down at the service station. It was a family business. I would take him home. He didn't have a car. My mother would give me 5 dollars for gas and lunch money for school. I would save most of it so I didn't eat very much for lunch. I would buy him some food. He never bought me anything. I was so nice to him. He didn't even offer to put gas in my car when I pick him up. Sometimes I would take him over to my mother house to visit. He worked with his family business so he could have some extra money for himself. He never did anything kind for me like going out to eat or the movies, I would have to be the one paying for everything.

One day he tried to have sex with me but I wouldn't let him. He shoved me down. I should have left him then. He never apologizes for pushing me down. He would get mad at me a lot for simple things. He always would break up with me for no reason. He kept me stressed out all the time. I would call him trying to get back with him. He said if he did I would have to start saving a bank for him. Like crazy I did. I would put change in it after a while it had cumulated up to 50 dollars. I told him I had a surprise for him that is when I gave him the bank I save for him. He took it and never showed any kind of emotion. I continued to buy him fast food. I was so young why would I let someone treat me in that manner

I got a job one summer. I was in the 11 grade now. We had been going together for a year. The summer job was only for two weeks. I was happy thinking about all the money I was going to make. After the summer job was over I received a check for two hundred dollars. I bought my boyfriend an outfit with some of the money: a pair of Levi jeans and an orange IZOD shirt. I thought that would make him like me more, I found out he allowed his little brother to wear his outfit. He had torn it up. He should have told me that he was going to let his family members wear it. I felt that it was not right. He did tell me that he was sorry, but really deep inside he wasn't.

It was prom time at my school. Oh, how I wanted to go. I had heard fun things about the prom. How you can get all dressed up

and look pretty. I loved dressing up. I just knew my boyfriend
would take me. One of his friends asked him if he was going to take
me to the prom. His friend had told me what he had said his
comment was HELL NO!!!!!! He was not taking me. Why I
thought he was ashamed of me. Everybody was going that I knew I
wanted to go so bad even my best friend was going. My feelings were
hurt and I thought that I was not good enough. I would always ride
him around in my car trying to be so nice to him. I wanted him to
like me the way I liked him. On the weekends, his mother would let
him drive her car around town he would go other places. He never
once ask me to go with him or even rode me around in his mother
car or come by to see me. When he had his mother car he would call
me when he came home .it was about 1:00 in the morning I would
be up waiting for him to call me. He always would tell me he was
going to play basketball with his friends. He had a cousin that was
over there with them. He would call me on the phone and tell me
everything that was going on. He told me that my boyfriend was
flirting with this girl. When I asked him he tried to deny it, but she
told other people that he liked her and wanted to go out with her. I
believe she was telling the truth. I saw her one day at school and I
asked her did my boyfriend like her. She responded yes and he calls
her all the time. Why did he lie to me? What was wrong with me, I
thought to myself. I found out she was not the only one he likes.
One day during P.E I overheard this girl telling her friends that her
and my boyfriend had sex. She showed her friends all the hickeys he
had put on her neck. I ran to the bathroom and cried. I asked him

after school did he have sex with this girl people were talking about. He talked about how ugly she was, but really she was ugly. About three days later the truth came out. I remember he said he was itching really badly. I started to think what it could be. He asks me if I could help him find something for the itching. He said he believes he had got something bad because it would not stop itching. He asks me is there anything he could use to stop the itching. I told him to go to the doctor. He ask me to go to the store and get him some medicine he said he could not take the itching anymore. He said he could feel something crawling on him. I asked him what is wrong with you. He never did answer. I said did you have sex with that girl. Why did you lie to me? What kind of person are you? That girl must if been a nasty person. He probably caught something from her. I am glad I never had sex with him. I remember what the girl said in P E to her friends. He had lie to me he did have sex with her. He didn't care about what I thought. He truly was a monster and caught something. He had the nerves to ask me to go to the store and get him some medicine for his nasty problem. He was to shame to go himself. I went like a crazy person to the store looking for something. I told the pharmacist what was going on they recommended some kind of cream. I bought it for him. I was so shamed in that store. I was hoping they didn't think I had that. I took it to his house and gave him the medicine. I felt like he didn't care about me going to the store. He was too embarrassed to go himself. I felt so stupid. He did not care long as it wasn't him in there. Why did I not just let him go? That was an opportunity for me to cut him loose. It was like the devil kept me in bondage to him. Later he did admit to having sex with her. I never told anyone I was too ashamed. He was a cheater and a liar. He told me he would not mess with her again. Who knows he was so harsh and mean and I was so young at the age of 17. I didn't know how a girl was supposed to be treated. I wanted to have fun go places.

One time that I can recall I was at school and someone asks him where was I at because there was something they wanted to tell me.. He pointed at the garbage can. The guy who asks about me knew my friend. She told me about what she had heard. She said to me your boyfriend thinks of you as nothing. That is how she felt. I still did not get the hint that this guy just did not care about me. I really wish I could have love myself and not look for love in all the wrong places. I was so desperate for someone to be nice to me. I was just blind to all the negative he offers me instead of love. I didn't ask him about it. I just kept quiet.

One day I picked him up from his mother and stepdad gas station. I took him home so he could change into some clean clothes. I waited for him to get dress. He finally got dress and we decided we were going to Popeye's to get something to eat. We order a carryout and brought it back to my mother house to eat. He got mad at me because I asked him a question about the girl he had sex with. Why did he lie about it? I told him he was not any good and he treats me badly and he uses me for his own selfish reason. We both were eating we had a two-piece white meat with fries. We had stopped by a

30

vending machine and got an orange soda to drink. He took the orange soda that I was drinking and poured it all over my chicken. All I could see was orange soda. My chicken was destroyed. I didn't have anything to eat. I sat there and watch him eat his chicken. He had no remorse. I told him he was evil! I was so angry at him then he grab me and started choking me with both hands. I could not do anything I felt my self-losing consciousness. He said my eyes were going back in my head. He was killing me, and my mother was in the other room. She heard a noise and ran into the living room and found his hands around my neck. That is when he turned me a loose. I remember running through the house screaming. I felt like pins were sticking all over my body I could not control myself. I ran in the kitchen and jumped on top of the washing machine I don't know why I did that. She went back in the room and ask him what did you do to that girl he said I did not do anything. My mom did not know that he was trying to kill me he took off running from my house. My mother did not do anything about what he had done to me or even take me to the doctor. she should have told me to leave him alone but she didn't. Wow, what a night. He was easy to get mad. All I wanted to do is make him happy.

One summer day as we were riding in my car I asked him a very simple question. Next thing I knew he took his hand swung it across the car to the passenger side where I was sitting. POW!!!!!! He slaps me in the nose blood was coming out my nose fiercely. I could not stop it from bleeding. I did not have a towel or anything I tried using my shirt to stop the bleeding. Blood was all over my face and my clothes. I told him don't hit me anymore. He told me to shut the fuck up and take him home. I cried and cried because there was so much blood on my face and clothes. I asked him what will I tell my mother. I asked him, why did you hit me? He said you should have shut your mouth He walked off and did not look back. I was sad as I drove home. He did not care. I went inside the house. My mom was in the living room. She asked what happen to my nose. I said you know how I have nose bleeds. She said did your friend guy hit you in the nose. I replied of course not. Finally, my nose stops bleeding. I washed all the blood off my face and changed my bloody clothes. I looked in the mirror to see if my nose looks crooked. It was ok. Thank God it was not broken.

That night he called me on the phone. He acted like nothing had happened. I asked him did he remember hitting me in the nose. He responded yea but your mouth is what gets you in troubledWhat could I have possibly done to make him that angry? He would always cut me off when I try to ask him a question. He never apologized for hitting me in the nose. I felt so bad when I was around him. I was so kind and nice to him. I felt as if nothing was good enough, but God protected me.

Christmas time came again. I asked my boyfriend to give me a ring for Christmas. He said ok all my friends were getting a promise ring from their boyfriends. I was so excited I went shopping for Christmas. My grandmother gave me 100 dollars to spend. I thought I was rich. I went to the mall. I was going to get him a nice

Christmas gift I saw a pretty coat I thought he would be happy to get. The price was kind of high. I knew if I bought him the coat I could not buy anything for myself. I really wanted him to have it. I spent all my 100 dollars on the coat. I just wanted him to have a happy Christmas. When Christmas day came we exchanged gifts. I could not wait to get my box. I hurried up and opened it. I was so disappointed. He did give me a ring but it was old fashioned and scratched up. I went from happy to sad. I wonder where he bought it from. It did not look new. It was his turn to open up his gift. He opens it and saw a brand new coat he smile, but I wasn't happy. I didn't tell him I didn't like the ring. I didn't want him mad at me. What a bad Christmas. I had used up all of my money my grandmother had given me on my boyfriend. All I got was an old scratched up promise ring. When Christmas break was over it was time to go back to school. All my friends had rings from their boyfriends. Everybody showed their rings off. Theirs was new shiny and pretty. They asked me to see my ring. I was so embarrassed. They looked at it and didn't say a word. I felt like my ring was very ugly. That is all I had for Christmas because I had used up all my Christmas money to get him a brand-new coat all I had was that old ring but he sported around with his new coat at school what a Christmas present I had. Later I found out he purchased it from the pawn shop.

Oh, how I wish someone would have told me about boys and having an education. During my high school years, my focus was on how I look. I never study like I should. Nobody told me how important school was. I should have done better. My boyfriend was one grade higher than me. I was in the 11 grade now he was a senior. I should have been a senior as well but I failed the 8th grade. He graduated from high school on his graduation all I wanted to do is be with him and make him happy. I wanted him to feel the same way about me.

It was time to go back to school I wanted a new look. My senior year I dyed my hair red. I thought it looked nice on me. My boyfriend saw my hair and said it did not look right. He likes it better black. I kept my hair red for a while. My hair started breaking off. So, I decided to dye it back black. He would always talk about this one girl in school. He would tell me she look like Mrs. America but she was not that pretty. I continued to talk to him even though I was miserable. I wanted him to like me and so I stop taking my birth control pills. I got pregnant in October 1984. I told him he didn't say a word. He told his mother she was very upset. My mom didn't seem to care either. As the months went by I started showing my tummy was getting bigger. I remember my PE teacher start asking me question about who the father of my baby was. One thing she said to me I never forgot to this day was my daughter were going to follow my footsteps and she was going to get pregnant at an early age just like I did. I never told anyone

My mother took me down to the welfare office for assistance. I started getting a check. I was just doing what my mother said to do. I received a check for 109.00 dollars every month. The lady at the welfare office asks me who the father of the baby was. I asked her why she wanted to know that. She told me that they are not the ones to take care of me he was.

I remember when I got low on money, I would ask him for some money. He never tried to help me knowing that I was pregnant with his child.   Once I bought a dress that I thought was so pretty. I showed him my dress he told me not to wear it to school. I wore it anyway because I liked it so much. He came up to the school when school was over. He sat in the parking lot with his cousin just to see if I wore the dress to school. I saw him just before I open the door to leave he was sitting in the parking lot waiting for me to come out. I stayed inside. I was scared.   I was very worried because he told me not to wear it to school.I wanted him to leave. Finally, he left because I never came out of the school. That night he called me and said he knew I had worn that dress that is why I didn't come out of the school. He hung the telephone up and did not talk to me for a few days.   Every time I tried to call him he would tell his mother to say he was sleep.

Two months later I gave the lady at the welfare office my boyfriend name. I believe they contacted him because he said he was going in the air force. He went and took the test and passed. He was scheduled to leave for basic training in May 1986. I was sad he was going to be leaving me. He said he was going to marry before he went to basic training. I was happy as months went by. My baby in my tummy was growing. It was fun being pregnant. For a while, toward the end, I was tired of being pregnant. He never said he was happy. I know now he wasn't. When the month of May roll back around the next year, it was time for him to leave for basic training. I remember taking him to the bus station, so he could go to the airport to fly out to Texas. We both were 18 at that time. He didn't marry me before he left. I was so sad that day, I remember crying seeing that Greyhound bus leaves with him on it. I stood by my car to watch him leave. I was waving to him: he never looked my way. I was 7 months pregnant at that time he left. I had two months left before the baby was born. I would have to go the doctor once a month for a checkup just to see how my baby was progressing. The doctor said at 9 months I would have to go every week until it was born. The doctor would listen to the heartbeat he said the heartbeat was strong and it sounds like a boy heartbeat. I didn't want to hear that because I wanted a little girl. I was due in July. I wished he could have married me before he left. I didn't know if we were going to still be together or not. I was hoping during basic training he would write me letters.

I would write him almost every day telling him how much I missed him. He would write back. I would ask in my letters to him did he miss me. He said he did. I still wanted to get married. I was hoping we did when he got home from his training. One day I had started slacking up writing. I wasn't missing him as much anymore. I believe I had started getting over him. He asks me why he was not getting letters from me like he uses to. He was in training for 6 weeks and after training he was sent to Texas for his job assignment. I was surprise my feeling had started to change toward him. I didn't feel the same way I use to, but even though I knew how I was feeling I started back writing him letters like I did before.

My mom was sick with cancer and I was eight months pregnant. She was in the Vanderbilt hospital in Nashville Tn. I was at the house by myself. I would go over my grandmother house for dinner. I hated I had to stay by myself. My uncle was still staying there with her. I didn't want to be around him anymore. He was so mean. I was praying that he didn't bother me or try to hit me while I was there. I packed a suitcase with all of my things I would need while in the hospital. As time went by, I started to get tired even more now being pregnant. Finally, I was 9 months. On July 4, I started having cramps. So I drove over to my grandmother because I was scared being by myself. My grandmother called my middle sister on the phone. My mother was in the hospital. They drove over and took me to the hospital but the doctor said I was having false labor pain. I was so disappointed. I was so ready to have my baby I had to walk with a walking cane. I could not lift my left leg or barely got off the bed.

I was worried about my mom. I didn't know if she was going to live or die. I didn't get to see her she was two hours away. My step father was with her in Nashville. He stayed with her the whole time. It was lonely being by myself. Sometimes I would stay at my grandmother house when my uncle was not there. Sometimes my boyfriend would call me. His mother never called call me to see how I was doing. She didn't even check on the baby. On the 7th of July, I spent the night at my grandmas. Since I did not feel very well and she thought I should not be alone anymore. About 5:30 am that morning I started having very bad cramps in my stomach. Grandma called my sister to take me to the hospital. I remember getting my suitcase out of my trunk of the car waiting for her to pick me up. When she got there my cramps were getting worse it took my breath away it hurt so badly. I got in the back seat of my sisters car down the street we went across the railroad tracks to the hospital. when I got there the doctor checked me to see if I was dilating, sure enough, this time was the real thing. I was admitted in the hospital, my sister said she would be back. I was all alone by myself with no family members and my boyfriend was away in the military. OH BOY!!!!!! I thought to myself this was terrible cramps after cramps I was having I could not get an epidural shot until I had dilated 4 centimeters. I could not wait.

The nurse came in and gave me an enema. When she gave me that enema, I had to use the bathroom right away. While sitting on the toilet, I had a contraction at the same time I had a bowel movement. The pain was so bad I was unable to sit on the toilet. I fell off the toilet on the floor. Poop went everywhere, my gown was messed up. I could not get up until that contraction was over. When it stopped I got up walk back to my bed. The nurse noticed that my gown was messed up. I changed into a clean one. I was so ashamed of the mess I made in the bathroom.

My pains were getting closer. I remember turning my head from side to side in pain. The nurse said, "I would be so glad when this is over for you, you are so young." The doctor came in and checked to see if I had dilated 4 centimeters so I could get my shot. It was about 7:30 that morning. I still haven't seen any of my family. I was alone. The doctor said the time was ready for the shot. I was so happy because I would not be able to feel anything from my waist down. That shot would numb me temporary till the baby was born. the doctor told me to lean forward on the side of the bed so they could give me a shot in my spine I had to be very still because I didn't want to be paralyzed from moving and getting that shot in the wrong area of my spine. The doctor said for me to bend over as I started to bend I had another contraction. I told the doctor to wait. I bent over across the bed the doctor said for me to be very still so I did that needle went in my back close to my spine my lower body started to feel numb. I could not feel anything from waist down. I was still having contractions, I just could not feel them. I would look at the monitor and see that my contraction was getting closer and closer together. It was a minute a part now. I was so glad I could not feel them anymore. I wish someone was there with me. I was sad.

I didn't know what had happened to my sister. She told me she was coming back. My mom was sick, and my boyfriend was away in basic training. The doctor came in to see how far I had dilated. I was at 9 centimeters. Thank God I was ready for delivery. They rolled me out the room. My time had come. I was still sad that I didn't have anyone there with me but I was happy to have my baby. I was so excited to find out what I was having a boy or girl. I wanted a girl. When I got in the delivery room, I remember seeing a big round mirror in front of me. They put my legs in something. My legs were spread far apart. Thank God I could not feel those contractions. The doctor told me to push as hard as I could. I had a hard time. The baby did not want to come out, so the doctor had to pull the baby out by its head using the forceps.

The big moment had arrived it was a girl. I was so happy, I wanted a girl hooray!!! The doctor gave her to me to hold. She was still bloody but I didn't care. She weighed 7 1/2 pounds. Wow, what a big baby. After the doctor cleans her up and stitched me up, the nurse rolled me and my baby to the recovery room. I was holding her very close to me. As we rolled down the hospital hallway I saw my sister. She came up to me and wanted to see her niece. She looked and didn't say anything. After I was in the recovery room the doctor put me in a room. I was happy it was over and I had a little baby girl. She cried a lot she kept her two fingers in her mouth. I stayed in the hospital for three days. The doctor wanted me to stay in the hospital for a longer time as I was having issues with my bladder. While I was pregnant the baby was pressing on my bladder this is why I was walking with a cane. My sister got in touch with her daddy mother to let her know that I had the baby. No one in his family came to the hospital to visit me. When my three days were up, my sister picked me and the baby from the hospital and drove me to my mother house. As I was carrying my little baby she was so little all wrap up in her blanket still sucking her two fingers, her point and middle finger. I could not wait to talk to my boyfriend about our baby girl. He finally called 5 days later. He was excited as well. I told him her name and how much she weighed. He said he could not wait to come back to see her. I took pictures of her and sent them to him.

My mother was still sick in the hospital with cancer. No one was at her house but my baby and I. I really did miss her. My dad spent most of the time with my mom at the hospital. She had to have chemotherapy. My step dad would come home just to get a change of clothes and go back to the hospital. He got to see my baby girl. He told me to take a picture, so he could show my mom.

She did not look like me. When she was born she looked a lot like her dad. Her head was dented a little bit on the side from the forceps when the doctor pulls her to the world. I knew as she got older it would go away. My mom would call sometimes to see how I was doing. She asks about the baby. I knew we didn't have a very close relationship as mother and daughter, but I did not want anything to happen to her. I wish I knew when she was coming home. I had no ideal. Finally, my boyfriend's mom came over 10 days after she was born. She brought her a bag of clothes. They were some used clothes. I had no ideal where she got them from. When I open the bag I found some girl dresses they were so big they were a size 4T. She was a newborn. She could not wear those clothes. It was the size to fit a four-year-old girl. What in the world was she thinking? I did not have any help with her but thank God I was getting some assistance. When I did get some money from assistance I would always buy her clothes and made sure she had plenty of diapers. She cried a lot. I believed her tummy was hurting. My grandma said she thinks she has colic. My mother finally came home from the hospital. Her skin looks dark and she was completely bald. Her hair came out from having chemotherapy treatment. She was very sick and weak. She didn't eat much because she did not have an appetite. Even though she was sick she wanted to hold her.

My little baby was getting bigger. I would take pictures of her and send them to her father. I could not wait to see him. He asked me to come to Texas to visit him while he was in training. I told him I had to wait 6 weeks until I was well. My baby did not have any hair people thought she was a little boy. So I got her ears pierced to make her look like a little girl. I remember one day a girl from school came over to see my baby. They said she looks just like her dad same color and everything. She never said she was cute. When she left she came back with 5 more girls to see her. They sniggle and laugh. I felt like they were making fun of her and thought she was ugly. I knew she was not a friend. She was my enemy. She was now w eeks old. She had her six weeks checkup we both were doing well. I wanted to see her dad, I really did miss him. It has been 3 months now since I saw him. I decided to go to Texas. I found a great deal on a bus ticket round trip. So I paid for it with some of the money I was getting every month. I was leaving for the weekend to see him. My mom kept the baby. She said she felt better. I was so excited to see him again. My sister took me to the bus station. I had my luggage all pack ready to go. I remember being so cold on that bus. I didn't bring a blanket. I didn't know the bus was usually cold. It was a very long ride to Texas. It was about 12 hours. It was long and cold. I couldn't wait to get to Texas. I was so cold, I never forgot how I was trembling. Finally, I arrived my boyfriend met me in a cab at the bus station. We rode back to the hotel close by the base. I was very happy that day. We gave each other a great big hug. I thought I was something. I had a military man. There was a pizza place across the street. We went out to eat. I was surprised that he paid for it. I thought maybe he had changed, at last, he looked different. All his hair was cut short. When he left he had curl, he looked better with his military haircut. We ate so much pizza. We both were stuffed. We went back to the hotel that I was staying at. He could not stay he had to stay on base so I stayed by myself it was lonely being there. I was only there for the weekend. He would come over after his training to see me. I called my mom to let her know I had got there. I ask her how was my baby doing. She said she was doing fine. I told her I would call her later to check on my baby. He said he wanted to marry me when he came home in November. I was starting to get sick my stomach. It was my bladder I had to drink cranberry juice after I had my baby. The last month of my pregnancy she was pressing on my bladder. It was hard for me to urinate. After she was born the doctor had to insert a catheter inside me. I thought I was well. I had my 6 weeks checkup. I was really hurting I could not even urinate. I was so ready to go home so I could drink some cranberry juice. My stomach was really hurting. He went back to the bus stop to see me off. I was headed back home it was cold again on the bus and I was in so much pain. I could not wait to see my home town. All I could think of was that cranberry juice. I hurt worse than when I was in the hospital. It was such a long trip back. I just laid my head on the seat in pain waiting to get back home. I wanted a blanket so bad I was so cold on the bus. I finally went to sleep and when I woke up and saw a sign that said t exits from my hometown. I was finally home my middle sister was waiting for me at the bus. She was about 21 years old now. I told her that I was in so much pain and I could hardly walk. I should have gone to the doctor. All that traveling I just wasn't quite healed from having problems with my bladder. When I went to my mother house I ran over to the kitchen and drunk me some cranberry juice. My baby was asleep. I missed her so much. I was glad to be back home. Looking back I should not have went to Texas even though I was released from the doctor. I was glad my mom was better. She was beginning to look like herself again. My baby was just getting bigger. Her hair was still slowly growing. She was still pretty.

It was almost time for my boyfriend to come back home. He said we would get married when he returned. He would finally get to see his little girl face to face for the first time. I was happy. He had been gone about 6 months. I sure did keep my daughter nice and pretty. I love buying her pretty things to wear. I could not wait until her hair starts growing. I would try to put her hair in a barrette and it slid right off. I knew someday her hair would be long and beautiful.

Sometimes I would go visit my grandmother. My uncle would always be there. He was still up to his same shenanigans: drunk, cursing and fussing. He would always say ugly mean things about my baby. Once, he said why you brought that ugly bitch over here. He still was up to the same old stuff year after year.

Most of the time she was sleep when he was using bad words. I was so glad she was just a baby and did not hear or understand those words. My uncle was still the same abusive person even toward a little baby infant that God created. I wanted to go visit my grandma a lot, but I didn't want to be there if he was there. When I told my mother what had happened. She didn't have any words to say about what I told her. My grandpa was the only person that ever treated me with love. I wish he was still alive but he died years ago. If I only could have had a few more years to spend with him. God knows best. He makes no mistakes.

Yippee one week until my boyfriend comes home, I was very excited. I was counting the days down until he was here. I wished he could have help me financially with our baby he never sent any money home for us. I didn't have any financial help with her not even from her father. The only help I had was from assistant which was 109 dollars a month and WIC. If I didn't have that my God what would I have done? God made a way for me and my baby. I didn't even realize it. The day came her dad was coming home. It was the end of October. I was really happy to see him. He called me from his mom house and told me he was here. I hurried got the baby and I together. Once I got to the house, I blew the horn for him to come out. Beep, beep! Finally, I saw him he look even different from when I saw him in the summer. He was kind of cute I thought. He walked over to the car and open the door. His daughter was in her car seat in the front seat. As he sat on the passager side his little girl was in the middle between us. He looks at her. It was his first time seeing her. He just stare and didn't say a word. He grabs hold of her little finger and held on tight. I was happy on that day. I was amazed how different he looks with his hair short. I was wondering in my mind was he really going to marry me. I wasn't going to mention it. I really just didn't care anymore. Maybe I was growing up some. I was going to wait for him to mention it. He had three weeks of leave time before he would be leaving. He was a station in Arizona. That was a long way from my hometown. I never really heard of Arizona. I just knew it was somewhere. Over the three weeks, we saw each other every day. He was scared to hold her. He thought he would drop her. I put her in his arms and told him to keep both arms around her. She was sucking her two fingers while he held her. She looks into his eyes. It almost like she knew he was her daddy. As time went by getting closer for him to leave he did not mention anything about getting married. I was not going to mention it either. I didn't even care anymore.

On the last week, he mentions us getting married. I said ok great. We went to the courthouse to get a marriage license. I told my mom that we were getting married. She asks me did I want to get married at her house. She said she would call the pastor at the church we attended, but for some reason, I did not want to be married in her house. I didn't want her to see me get married. It was like I was not comfortable with her seeing me. So since I didn't agree she said she know another minister who could marry us. She gave me the phone number. I called him he ask when did I want to get married. I told him the next day if he was not busy. My boyfriend told his mother we were getting married. She said to him that she didn't think that was a good ideal because when times get hard I would run back home to my mother. If she went to the wedding she would stop it. They had got into an argument about a driveways years ago. Her in-laws used to stay next door to my grandmother and they had to share the driveway. Ever since that happens she never did like my mother and I guess that is why she didn't want her son to marry me. I wasn't born when that incident happen. It was a long time ago. I could not believe what his mother had said. I was so surprised at her being that way. I didn't know she was that terrible. I didn't do anything to her or her son for her to think of me in that way. I always use to think about that from time to time.

The next day came. It was time to get married. I asked my best friend would she come and be a witness. She said she would I got all dress up I thought I was looking good that day. I forgot what he had on.   I had on a pretty blue jean skirt and a shirt.   It was my day as we drove over to the minister house to get married. We knock on the door his wife ask us to come in.   We went into their living room where he performs our ceremony. The minister was really old. I did not know he was such an old man like that. I wish I had allowed my mother to ask her pastor to marry us.   We could not understand anything he said. He stuttered so bad it was funny. I wanted to laugh. All I could understand he said at the end that y'all can set it up.   I guess we were married.   We finally got hitched. As we drove away I was happy that day.

We went back to my mother house.   He did not stay with me at her house. He had to stay at his mother house. I thought that was bad. We were married and could not stay together. My mom was not going to let him stay there. She said when yawl get your own house than you and he can stay together.   I thought that was so mean of her. It was time for him to go back to the military. We only had two days left together. I thought we were not going to get married but we did. We were a family. That is all I ever wanted. I was excited that his daughter had his last name.

When the day came for my husband to return to his work assignment in Arizona,   he had asked this funeral home, which was a friend of our family to drive him to the airport. I was going with him as well to see him off to the airport. When he left that morning he was nervous. We had to pull over every 20 minutes so he could go to the bathroom. I was so embarrassed. I guess he was as scared, as we went inside the airport. It was very big. That was the first time I had ever been to an airport. After he checked in, we all sat down and waited for his flight to leave. Finally, his flight number to Arizona was called. They were boarding now. I was sad to see him leave. I cried a little. I waited in the window until his plane had left. I knew it would not be long until we were together again. We drove back home. I cried to myself softly thinking that day when we would be all together again. As time went by, my husband would call to tell me he was looking for an apartment and a car. That made me excited. I was going to be living so far away from home and I was only 20 years old. I have never been that far before but it didn't matter, I wanted to be with him. I was hoping he had changed and was not abusive anymore.

I notice the next month I didn't receive any assistance. What had happened I thought? I never told them I had got married. How did they find out? So I decided to call them and ask what had happened. I was not warned I was going to be cut off. I didn't receive a letter in the mail. The lady at the office said she knew I was married. I ask her how she knew. She said she saw my name in the newspaper. I only have been married four weeks. I didn't think that was true. A lot of people could have had that same name. I thought for a long time my mother-n-law must have called them since I thought she didn't like me. I started to think why would she be that mean. I told my mother about it, she was very quiet. My grandmother thought it was very awful for someone to do that. I always wonder who really called and turn me in. One day it came to me over the years who it was. I realized who, and I was surprised I figured it out it had to be someone close to me for them and the lady at that office to believe them. I was stunned when I found out the truth. My mother did tell them. My grandmother said they called my mother house for something and asked for me and my mother told them I was married. They called for something else. She volunteered and told them. I don't know her reason. She told them but maybe she did not want me and her granddaughter to receive an assistant anymore. God was always with me. Every time I thought about it I got sad because I asked her about it and she did not tell me that she told them. I would think how I missed my grandpa if only he was still living my life would have gone a different path.

The day came when it was time for me to leave to go to Arizona to join my husband. I was very happy that day. I had packed all my things for me and my little girl. I was kind of nervous about riding on an airplane with the baby. I was hoping she would not cry on the plane so I packed her a lot of bottles to keep her full and sleepy. I had to leave my car at my mother house, but I was ok with that since my husband had already bought a car. I couldn't wait to see our new apartment. That day when I left I hugged my grandma, mother, and sister goodbye. I asked my mother to come to the airport with me since the funeral home guy was going to drive me to the airport. she said she would go. Upon arriving at the airport, when I got all checked in. my mom never said she loves us or she would miss us. She just looked. When it was time for me to board the plane, I told my mom goodbye. I was sad to be leaving my hometown to a place I never been. I was 20 years old when I left. We didn't say we love each other or anything or give each other a hug.

When I arrived in Arizona, my husband met us at the airport. He had brought a pretty white car. It was a Celebrity with 4 door .we didn't have a car seat for the baby, all we had was a baby carrier. I buckle her down in the car and we drove off from the airport. Arizona was different from where I was from. There were so many tall mountains all around. I was so surprised to see orange trees with oranges on them. There was also tall palm trees. I never seen such a sight. As we kept driving along the road I saw a cactus. Oh wow! It was beautiful. When we arrived at our apartment, I was anxious to see the inside. I got out with our baby and walk to the door. I wanted to see what it looked like inside. When he opened the door I looked around it was small. It came fully furnished. It was a one bedroom apartment. It was kind of cute. We didn't have any supplies for our place. We didn't have any sheets, pots, and pans. We didn't have anything.

I unpacked all of my clothes and put them away. We needed hangers to hang our clothes. My husband didn't make a lot of money, he was an airman at that time. He had to take care of us the best way he could. It was 7 days until he got paid. We were very hungry. He had a few dollars so we bought some bologna and bread to for me to eat. He had a meal card to eat on the base. He would eat there every day. I also had a few starbursts. I could not eat a lot of it because I didn't want to run out of food. That was the only thing I had to eat. I divided the candy and bologna. I was so hungry. Thank God our daughter stayed full. God was watching over us. I called my mother to tell her that we didn't have any money until he got paid. I asked if she could send me a few dollars so I didn't have to be hungry. She fussed at me, but she sent 20 dollars by Western Union. I got it the same day. I didn't know why I gave that money to him, I was hoping we would get something good to eat. I was so hungry he decided to go to a gas station and get us a lemon box pie and put some gas in his car with some of the money. I wanted something good to eat so badly. I never said anything to him about what he did. There was a little change left but he kept it for himself. I use to wonder why we had to eat at a gas station. We had only a few days left until he got paid. We needed so much stuff for the house. We just didn't have enough money. They had an Airman attic for people who didn't have enough money on the base for military families .they had clothes, household good, and other things that were donated for families that did not have much. I would go there weekly just to see what they had. Sometimes they had nice things and sometimes they didn't. I found some plates and forks at the Airman attic. Finally, the day came to go to the grocery store we got some supplies we needed. I am glad we were able to get some towels and sheets and food to eat. I was so thankful that my baby never went hungry. She always had plenty of milk.

One weekend morning, I decided I didn't want to put my

clothes on. So I just laid on the floor with my gown on. I thought I was covered up. I thought he had changed from being bad toward me. He told me to go and put on some clothes. I just kept laying there on the floor. I would not get up since I would not listen to what he said he decided to get me up and started hitting me. I didn't understand I thought he had changed. He was being very mean. I thought here he goes again. All I was doing was just lying on the floor in our own house. He hit me until I got up. I ran in the bedroom and locked the door. I cried and got so sad he never told me he was sorry. I didn't say anything to him the rest of the day. I was so scared.

It was almost Christmas in 1985 my mother in law called and asked to speak to me. She said she was sorry for what she had said about me and asked me to forgive her for saying when times get hard that I would leave the marriage. I was shocked but I forgave her. Our baby was 5 months old. His mother sent us our Christmas present. She sent a check to us and she told him to give me and the baby 50 dollars each. Instead, he kept the entire check and didn't give us anything. I called and told his mother. She said the next time she was going to send our present separate since he was taking it for himself. God supplies all of my needs even though he kept our portion of our Christmas money, God never left us. The week before Christmas I went to the airman attic and found my little girl some small toys she could play with. I wanted a Christmas tree so bad, we didn't have the money to get one. It kind of made me sad thinking about how he took our money. We could not have a tree or

Christmas presents. I told myself one day we will have a tree and toys. Finally, it was Christmas although it didn't seem like itIt felt like an ordinary day. I knew it was Christmas. He was mean on that day and I was always nice to him. I thought on Christmas everybody should be happy. We didn't exchange gifts because he said he was the only one working. But I had my baby some toys.

It was now New Year's Eve he went to sleep pretty early that night, maybe around 9 o'clock. I wanted to us to stay up together to see the new year come in. So my baby and I were up so we watched TV Times Square in New York. I wanted to watch the ball drop at midnight it was almost there 5 4 3 2 1 Happy New Year! It was 1986 a New Year. I was hoping this year I could get a job so we could have more money. It was a new place on the air force base that was opening up, a Burger King Restaurant. I saw where they were taking applications .so I went to pick me one up after filling out the application, I turn it back in hoping they would call me for a interview. Finally, the phone rang after a week. I pick it up hello you have an interview for a position that you applied for. Would you be interested coming in for an interview? I said yes oh yes I hung up the telephone so happy. Thank you, God I said I got my call I prayed for.

I went to the interview. They hired me right on the spot. It was my first job. I was so proud of myself. I was so happy. I told my husband about it he didn't seem that happy for me. I finally started working at Burger King. Sometimes I had to work at night, but it was ok because I didn't want to be broke all the time. It was hard for me working because I had a problem working the cash register and counting money. I wish I had done better in school. I tried but it was just hard. There is a reason for everything. I was so ashamed of myself around my co-workers. One day I had to work the drive-thru. I knew it was going to be hard for me counting back change to customers. I did it some kind of way. There was another worker I can still remember how she looks she laughed at me and told other coworkers there that I couldn't count back money. They laughed and laugh at me. I felt like a dumb-dumb. That made me feel so low. I told myself I was not going to be like that again.

My daughter was still on WIC because her daddy still was not making a lot of money. We really did need it and I was so thankful. One afternoon we went to Phoenix to one of the grocery stores to purchase her milk that accepted WIC. On our way back down the interstate, my husband was driving pretty fast maybe around about 70 miles. We were trying to hurry up. The green light was on yellow he tried to outrun it. He was driving even faster. I was so scared. I was holding my baby in my lap. She was about 6 months old now. I was holding her so tight OMG!!!!! We crash into this white truck. We hit it on the passage side me and the baby went into the dashboard of our car. My head hit the dashboard so hard but I never let her go. I held on so tight she was still in my arms. Her daddy hurts his knees pretty bad. I had a big lump on my forehead and our baby had a bad cut on her lip. Blood was everywhere. She was bleeding. I was scared. Her blanket was so bloody I could not stop the bleeding.

After the police arrived he gave my husband a ticket for running the red light and not having a car seat. We should have gone to the hospital to take our 6 months old. We all were hurt her lip finally stop bleeding that knot on my head stayed there for a month. I don't know why we didn't go to the hospital. We could have been killed. My head did hurt and so did his knee. The baby's lip was cut pretty deep. Her dad finally said if we had gone to the doctor, he would have got in trouble with the military for not having his daughter in a car seat. God was right there. He was our protection in the time of trouble. God kept her safe so she didn't go through the windshield. When I look at her it always reminds me of the wreck. The scar never went away but she was too young to remember.

I'm now 21 years old. My husband worked a lot of long hours. I was still working at Burger King. Our car was total from the accident. We didn't have a car at that time. We had to walk to work. It was not that far from the base. We lived on a busy highway. I had to work the hours he wasn't working. He worked nights and I worked days' and I had to work some weekends. On the weekends he would meet me half way with our baby in her stroller. I still remember what she had on a yellow long sleeve sweater and some blue jeans pants and white shoes finally we did get another car .it was a blue ford escort and it was 4 doors .it was not as nice as the other car but I was thankful to have a car.

One day my husband and I were arguing because he wanted to

control the money I made while at Burger King. He wanted to me to turn over the whole check and he was going to give me what he thought I should have. I told him I wanted to handle my check. Why did I have to give it over to him? The next thing I remember he took his hand and hit me in the face. I cried and cried. I gave it to him so he would not be mad at me. He told me that I was a complaining Bitch. It seems like every week he was mad about something. I didn't know what was wrong with him.

When Christmas rolled back around it was always bad on the holidays. He got our daughter some toys this Christmas. It wasn't a lot. I thought we would have a good Christmas day but instead, he was fussing about little things. Why didn't close the cabinet, you running to much water in the bathtub, just little things? I asked him why was he so mean. He yelled back and said there you go again running your mouth and shoved me to the floor. I got up and thought what I did so wrong to him, it Christmas. I thought in my mind he didn't say anything to me that entire day. I had cooked us a nice dinner to eat. My daughter was over a year old now. She had a weird look on her face she saw me hit the floor so hard. She just stared and started crying. I told her it was ok, I just fell.

She was so excited about her toys. She had a play cooking stove. She loved that stove. She also had a little broom and dustpan. She likes to play with the one in the house. She played all day with her toys that Santa brought her. We sat down and had our Christmas dinner. I sat her down first and fed her. She was very hungry from all that playing. After I fed her I fixed me and her dad plate. He was still in a bad mood. I never knew what was wrong with him .why was he not happy. I didn't want to ask him because I was afraid he would lash out at me again in front of my little girl.

Every New Year he would go to sleep early. it was like he was doing that on purpose . It was always me and my daughter awake to see the New Year come in. I wanted us to be a family. I always wanted that. It was lonely being in Arizona. I felt that way a lot. I didn't think marriage life was supposed to be lonely.

Finally, another year had passed by 1987. It was not very cold in Arizona during the winter months. The low was about 40 degrees. We had no snow there but there was a lot of mountains .all around tall ones that you could see from far off.

February was here. I remember one afternoon he came home for lunch. I had met this girl, her husband was also in the service. She would come over to visit. One day she knocks on the door. My husband was there. I went out my door to see what she wanted. She asked me if my husband could take a look at her car. It was stranded down the street. I went back inside to ask him if he would take a look at her car since he was good fixing cars and he told me No. I went outside and made an excuse not to tell her the real truth. She said it was ok and she would find someone else. I felt really bad about her car stranded and I knew he could have helped her. I told her I was sorry and returned to the house. When I entered the house he fussed and fussed at me. He told me not to ask him to do that again. I told him she needed help then he pushed me down. I began to cry and he picked up a shoe and came after me. I ran but he caught me. I jumped in the bed and I tried to get away but I couldn't and he took that shoe and began to hit me all over my body. He just kept hitting me over and over and finally, he left me alone. My daughter ran and hid. She was very scared and crying. He then put the shoe down and left. I remember my arms and legs were stinging from that shoe because he had hit me as hard as he hard as he could. I cried and cried with pain. I went to the bathroom and looked at my body in the mirror, and I was shocked to see shoe prints all over my body. It was so many over my arms, legs, and back. It was black shoe prints. Lord, there was so much pain. I needed you. I wonder and wonder why my husband hurt me so bad. I was now 21 years old with so many bruises so far from home. My daughter came out from hiding. she looked at me with a sad face and said mommy leave dad he hurts you. I was so surprised. She did not think I needed to be with her dad. When he returned home from work, he saw all the bruises on my body, and I ran up to him and said look what you did to me. I kept saying that over and over. I wanted so bad to pick up the most massive thing I could find and hurt him. He told me that I talk too damn much. I said I don't speak too much all you do is hit me over and over again. He was always angry like he hated me.

The temperature was getting hot in Phoenix, Arizona. It was such a pretty city full of mountains. I always wanted to go to the mountains but I knew my husband wouldn't want to. We lived on a busy highway. I think the speed limit was about 55 mph. One day my daughter and I were in the parking lot of our apartment. She took off running toward the highway. I could not catch her. I was talking to some neighbors in the parking lot. She was going straight on the highway and I was running trying to catch her, but I couldn't. I knew she was going to get run over. For some reason, she took a turn and went down the sidewalk. It was like angel guided her down the safe path. It was like a miracle because she was headed straight for the street. I was so scared she was going to get hit by a car but God kept her safe.

It was time for me to go to work at Burger King. I worked the hours he was home because I didn't trust anyone to keep my little girl. I was very cautious of her. One day I told my manager that I could not work the hours that he scheduled me to work. I was on the night shift and I wanted me to work days. he told me if I could not take the heat get out of the kitchen. I was fired that day. I had no job and my husband was not going to give me any money. When I would ask for money he would tell me I'm not your father. I remember not having any money. We would have to go to the laundry room to wash our clothes in our apartment complex. We didn't have a washer and dryer in our apartment. I didn't have any money so I asked him for some money. I think I wanted some chips and stuff. He said he would give me my part of the money that was used for washing clothes. I wanted some snacks so bad I said ok. I had to wash my clothes in the bathtub on my hands and I hung them up to drip dry in the bathroom. Why was my husband so mean?

I didn't have a job or any money. I had to depend on him for everything and I could not get my personal supplies. I would have to use toilet paper for my tampons. I was afraid of him, he was so cruel towards me. I could not ask him simple questions without him getting angry. He would call me stupid and dumb all the time. He never would tell me good things about myself and he always put me down. I would see a couple in the store and it seems like they were so happy. I wish that could be my life. I thought I was not good enough for him. I always tried to keep myself in top notch shape hoping that he would treat me better or notice the good things about me.

One day I met another friend. She lived very close to me in the apartment down the street. Her husband was in the military also. She had a little boy that was a year older than my daughter. We would talk on the phone. it seems like she was jealous of me because she always would tell me negative things that people supposedly said about me. I remember one thing that she said that someone said I had a big pie face. I never was a big person. I think weighed about 130 pounds. I was only 5'4. I didn't think I was that big but that comment she made continuously bothered me. From that day I started trying to lose weight. I would walk around my apartment complex several times. I did not want to have a fat face. She said other people were saying that as well. I watched what I ate constantly. I started losing weight but it was hard starving myself. I really did miss eating some of the things I liked. One day as I was watching Oprah Winfrey show. The topic of the day was about eating disorders. It was a lady on TV that was bulimic. She shared her story how she once weighed 50 pounds and almost died. She was recovering from her illness and now was weighing 80 pounds. She looked very bad but instead of making sure I didn't end up like her I did the opposite. I ended up trying to lose weight and still eat some of my favorite food so I started throwing up every time I would eat because I wanted to look great. I continued to throw up day after day. When my husband would come home in a bad mood and act mean towards me it would cause me to throw up worst. I had made a habit out of it now. I tried stopping but I just couldn't. I was now almost 23 years old and it was my third year living in Arizona. He was always quiet around me. We never went anywhere together. We stayed at the house, it was so boring and lonely. I didn't talk to my family a lot.

One weekend while at home he complained about everything all day. I got so tired of hearing it he was polishing his shoe. I told him that I didn't want to hear it anymore. He started calling me bitches, hoes, stupid, and dumb ass. He said that's why your retarded self-don't have a job. I told him to shut up and he took that shoe polish and tried to put it in my eyes. I moved away just in time. He came after me and took his fist and hit me in the eye. My eye hurt so bad it was blurry to see. It started to swell and became black all around the eye. He had given me a black eye. I grabbed my little girl and ran in the closet she was scared I hugged her tight and told her I would take care of her and not let anything happen her. I prayed to God please, Lord make all this bad stuff go away. Oh God, I need you so bad. I could hear his voice outside of the closet calling me bad names and how crazy and dumb I was he even hit the closet door I thought he was coming after me again but I guess God was protection us.

I didn't tell anyone what he did to me. My little girl would look at me and say mommy why your eye is so black, is it because of what daddy did? I was so ashamed I didn't answer and she had a very sad face. She saw what her dad had done to her mom but didn't understand. I was hoping and believing he would change and be the husband I hope for, but my eye stayed black and swollen for almost two weeks. He never apologies for hurting me. I thought maybe if I could be a little nicer to him he would not hit me anymore. I wish my life was better than what it was. I felt bad and therefore I continued to throw up. I had an eating disorder that no one knew about. It was my secret. I would watch the 700 Club TV ministry hoping to find some comfort in God. I wanted God to protect me from the violence that was in my life. I knew of God but I never really tried to get to know him like I should have. I didn't attend any church while in Arizona but I knew God was real.

As time went by things did not improve for me. He continued to put me down. I would cook dinner hoping he would complement my cooking and he would eat it and say nothing. He never told me happy things. I made sure every day I combed my hair and put my make up on and I was fully dressed. I wanted to call my mother and grandma and tell them all the things he was doing to me but I didn't think they would care.

When my husband would go to work in the afternoon he would take the car and drive to the base. He worked on the flight line. When he left for work I didn't have any idea what time he would return. It was just me and my daughter sometimes it would be 2 or 3 o'clock in the morning before he would return home. I was very lonesome in Arizona. He didn't work weekend unless he was called in but most of the time he didn't. I didn't have a sex life. It was all about him. He never kissed me or anything. I always would do what he liked when we did have sex. He would just do what he wanted, I was just there. I wondered if that's how marriage supposed to be. I never liked to look at love stories on TV because it would make me mad that it wasn't me. Lord God, I wonder and wonder what I did so wrong in your eyesight to deserve this. I didn't want to have a life like this but didn't know what to do. One day when I was at the base commissary it was a guy there that gave me a compliment nice and it made me feel great inside.

My husband would always tell me he was going to break my nose right in the middle over and over again. My husband would always tell me he wishes he had married someone else he had saw in the military. I would think what was wrong with me. Wasn't I good enough? He said he had seen someone that he wishes it was her instead of me. I felt so bad to hear my husband tell me words like that. The more I heard those words the more I continued to exercise and throw up and watch what I ate. One day when we went to the commissary on the base which was the grocery store. I saw a woman in there that I just knew that she was the woman that he had in mind. She was also in the military. I ask him was that her when we get home and he finally told me that was her. What in the heck was wrong with the wife he already had? He did not appreciate me for who I was or how nice I was to him. I wish I could be the wife he wanted. Maybe someday I thought.

It was now Thanksgiving and we decided we decided to go back home for the first time since I have been in Arizona. I was glad to be in my hometown again. We drove all the way there. It was a long, tiring drive. It took 13 hours to get there. When we got there my mom didn't look very happy to see us. Well, we had Thanksgiving with my family. He didn't complain while we were there. Thank you, Lord. We had three weeks to be there. It was wonderful to be back in our hometown. I saw my grandmother and my two sisters and brother. None of us hugged when we saw each other. I haven't been home in a while. I was thinking to myself I will always hug and make my daughter feel welcome and loved. My mother had three bedrooms. The bedroom that she assigned to us was the bedroom with a full-size bed with plastic on the mattress. She didn't let us have a bedroom to ourselves. She said we all had to sleep in the little bed all three of us on the noisy thick plastic that was on the bed. I couldn't wait to go back to my home in Arizona. It just didn't make any sense. It was almost like she didn't want us to have any privacy.

Every time you moved around on the bed that plastic moved with us. That plastic made the bed hard to sleep on. We have to sleep in that tiny room all together with no closet space or drawer to put our clothes in. We lived out of the suitcase. She took the bathroom rug up so we didn't step on her rug when we got out the bathtub. We didn't have anything to dry our feet on. Also, she took all the toilet paper out the bathroom so we didn't use hers. It was horrible visiting with her. I just thought maybe things would have changed.

Finally, it was time to go back to Arizona. I was glad it was very hard living with her. It was almost like she did things on purpose. We loaded our car up and told everyone goodbye and headed down the highway back to Arizona. Driving back was very long. On our way back I had fallen asleep in the car. I remember he had his hand in my underwear. I woke up and ask what he was doing. He told me that he had put a penny in my vagina. I yelled and asked him are you crazy. I tried to get it out. my daughter was in the back seat of the car in her car seat I didn't want her to see what I was doing I took my hand to see if I could get it out. I got scared because I couldn't feel it so I had to take my hand and he had put it so far up in my vagina. I thought I was not going to find it. I thought it was lost. I was scare that I would get an infection. I asked him again why he did that to me. He said he wanted to see what it would be like to have a penny inside my body. I never told anybody what he had done.

We finally got back to Arizona. I was glad to be back in my own house. I was thinking I didn't know if I ever wanted to go back and visit again. The vacation that I thought that would be a great turned out to be horrible. I wish I had a loving mom that felt like a mommy.

I continued to keep my weight down. I didn't want to eat anything that would take me back to what I did not like to see on me. We didn't have a lot of money and only had one income. There was so much I wanted to do in my life. I wish I had a job so I could have my own money. I didn't like to ask my husband for anything. If I did have my own money he would take it.

It was income tax time, it was February now. I was hoping and excited about the tax money we were getting back 1300.00 dollars. I just knew he would share some of that money with me when we received our refund check in the mail. I asked him for a portion and he gave me 25.00 dollars out of 1300.00. When I ask him why my portion was only so small he replied you don't deserve anymore because you don't have a job so why should I give you more. He kept all that money for himself. I felt so bad. I wish he could of have given me more but I knew if I would have kept talking he would have hit me. It was almost like he wanted me to have just a little. He bought himself all kinds of stuff and me and my daughter didn't have anything.

Oh God help me, I was stressed and in so much pain. Help me my God take me to a place where misery is not there. Every time I didn't do things the way my husband would approve of he would make fun of me and call me names stupid, dumb, and ass bitch If I would call him a name back he would jump up in my face and threaten me. He would continue to tell me I'm going to break your nose. He pushed me and grabbed a spray bottle and sprayed water all over me. Every time I would try to say something he would spray water in my face and clothes.

One day as I was going to the mailbox it was a sign posted saying babysitting job. I wrote the number down and called. I was excited. I talk to the guy on the phone and he said he needed a babysitter and if I was interested I told him I would be more than happy. it was a Friday when I spoke with him. He asked me if his little boy could start Monday. He was a single parent and a military guy as well. He said he would bring him over around about 7:30 am and pick him up at 4:30 Monday through Friday. He said he would pay me $75.00 a week. I was very excited to have a little money for myself. I told my husband about the news he didn't say a word. Monday came and the guy brought him over as he said. He had all the things he needed to be packed in his bag. He was a cute little boy I think he was about 15 months. he was a busy little boy very curious about everything always messing with things in the house the TV, the refrigerator so on and so on. One day my husband was at home while I babysat this little boy. He didn't like how busy he was and he would put him in a little space surrounded by something I can't remember but it was for the little boy to not to get out and bother his things. I would say I thought it was our things together. He would always relate to his stuff as the little boy continued to come over. If he was there he would put him in that area so he would not get out.

I told him not to put that little boy in that area. He got mad and slapped me in the face and said go somewhere else and keep him because he was not going to allow him to walk around bothering stuff. I couldn't wait until he left so I could get him out that area.

One day he came home I was not expecting him so early. The little boy was out having fun even though he got into stuff he was only a baby. My husband saw he was walking around the house and he put him in that area. I told him to leave him alone he push me down and said this is my house. You don't pay any bills here so shut your damn mouth up, stupid bitch. I didn't say anything to him because I knew he would have hit me. So after that little boy was put back in that area so he could not mess with his things in the house. He wanted him to stay in there the entire time he was home. If he saw him trying to leave that area he would spray him with water. I wasn't going to put up with that anymore. I told his dad I could not keep his little boy anymore. I made up an excuse I just could not see a grown man spray a little one-year-old until he was soaking wet all over. My husband was a cruel evil man. I wish I knew more about him before I married him. He was the worst person I had ever met in my life. My God why me? Why so many tears? I lay awake at night imaging how it would be with a life full of love. Oh God help me because I need you so bad. I wanted someone to take me away from that kind of life. I wanted someone to love me and treat me with no pain.

I would always remember my grandfather how it felt to sit on his knee and be held in his arm. I just missed him so much and his love. One day he was being so nice to me I was wondering has he change maybe my prayer was being answered. Yippee, he said he was giving me some money so I could go to the mall. It sounded strange at first but maybe he is changing. So I took the money me and the baby we headed to the mall. I stayed for about a couple of hours and headed back home. When I got home my husband was there. I just got a strange feeling why all of a sudden he volunteered to send me to the mall. About two weeks later my next door neighbor which was an Indian, called me on the phone and said my husband was bothering her. She asks me did I remember the night when they had locked their keys in the house and when her husband had knocked on our door to see if your husband could help us well she said my husband was touching on her butt. One day when you left your husband called and asked if he could have sex with her. She just wanted me to know. I was so shocked and I couldn't wait until he got home from work. When he did I approached him and asked him he wouldn't answer. I told him that's why you sent me to the mall not that you changed but you were cheating and wanted me out the way. I told him why would you touch another women butt with her husband standing right beside him and she would have hit you or told her husband right on the spot what you did   I told him I was not stupid. He got so mad and punched me in the face and hit me in the eye, and then slung me to the floor. The carpet burned me on my face. The punch to my face caused me to have a black eye. He just walked away like he didn't care or have any feeling of what my face looked like. My suffering would not go away. I ask God to make it better for me and my daughter. I was so distressed and upset.

When everyone had gone to sleep, I ate as much as I could eat until my stomach was poked so far out and then after I felt so bad and fat. So I hurried to throw up all the food. I felt a release. My eye was black, and there was a burn from being beat into the carpet. He just couldn't apologize for the bad things he did to me over and over. He always blames me for everything that caused him to be angry. A couple of days later we went to a place to get a loan for a certain amount of money. I went with him in the car. I didn't want anyone to see my eye, so I put a bandage under my eye where the burn was. I was so ashamed for someone to see me like that, but I went anyway. The loan officer looked at me so hard with a stare. I guess he could tell something or someone had hit me in my face. I just couldn't wait to get out of there. it seemed like every week he was hitting me for something he said I was doing wrong. I wish I knew what to fix to make him happy. I didn't know what. I always would go in my closet and ask God to make him better and cry with so many tears. I was depressed I would throw up food. It didn't matter if it was a little or a lot. That's what made me feel better. Finally, those neighbors became enemies to us. One evening her husband came kicking at our door. He was trying to kick it open. The door was about to come apart it scared my daughter and me. He was screaming out his name. My husband was holding the door with his shoulders. But he was kicking the door so hard it was like it was coming apart. I was wondering what was going on, so I called 911 and call for help. He ran into the kitchen and got some salt. He said he was going to throw it in his face if he kicks our door down. I think our neighbor heard the policeman coming, so he left and went back to his house. The policeman came and asked what happen. I told him I think our neighbor was angry because he found out my husband had tried to have an affair with his wife. He said to me he would be mad himself who would not. He told him not to go over their house again bothering them, and he told our neighbor the same thing. Shortly after that, they moved away. I was glad. I didn't have to see them again I thought to myself why my husband would attempt to have an affair with this Indian woman that was much taller than him and very fat. The more I thought about that, the more I threw up because I wanted to be perfect. I always kept myself up. I thought that he would be satisfied with me, but I guess not. Dear God, please help me I'm not happy my peace and joy have been taken from me. Help me Jesus and cover me with your blood. Sometimes I wish that someone would take me far always from this life that I was in. On holidays, birthdays, and anniversary's he made them as sad as possible. I never understood why he would start up fights and arguments on special days and weekends. As time went by the more, I prayed nothing changed in my life. things stayed the same. I didn't have relatives to talk to for comfort I just had my daughter.

We were getting a new neighbor next door in the apartment

where the Indian family had moved out of. This couple was black. .One day when I went to the mailbox, I met the lady next door. We greeted each other and told each other our name. We became friends she had a teenage son. She was a nice lady. We began to talk and visit each other. One day she told me things about her life thing that happen to her. I was shocked to find out that she was an ex-prostitute and had been raped by two men. Also, she used crack cocaine even though she had things about her that I didn't do I continued to talk with her. We became close and talked even more. She was a friend of mines. He son was a little weird. He would take his family picture to other people in the apartment complex just to show them his family that was funny to me. One day the lady next door ask me to take her to someone's house because she didn't have a vehicle. I told her sure. I took her to her destination. When she got back in the car she told me she picked up some crack cocaine. I had my daughter in the car with us. I didn't know about drugs. As I think now I could have gotten in some bad trouble as being a young woman. I just didn't know.

One day I took my neighbor to the store. My husband had put a sign in his car that said no smoking. She took out a cigarette and started smoking in the car. I knew my husband would have gotten mad about her smoking but for some reason I didn't stop her. My heart was beating so fast.I was scared to the tell her to stop. I was praying God, please let this smoke be out this car, but maybe I should have said something, but I was frozen and could not tell her to stop. When we arrived at our apartment, I kept the window down for a while trying to air out the car. Finally, the smell was gone. I was afraid that my husband would find out. The next day when he took the car to work and when he returned home he asked me did someone smoke in his car. He always said everything was his stuff, and I couldn't say anything I was so scared, but he continued to get angry at me for the smoke he had smelled. He walked towards me, and I took off running to the bathroom and lock the door, so he could not come in. he got some tools and took the lock off the door. I tried to hold the door closed as long as I could but he pushed it open and started to hit me and punched me in my face and head over and over again. my daughter was running trying to stop him. I told her to run and hide. She tried to keep her dad from hitting me. She tried to pull him off of me screaming dad leave mommy alone. I could not do anything. He called me a stupid bitch and said did I not tell you not to let anyone smoke in my car. Did you not see the sign that I had in the car do not smoke sign. He grabbed a monkey wrench about half the length of my arm and stood over me and had it drawn back. I thought I was going to die. He said to do it again and see what else happen the next time. He took that wrench and hit the top of the door and slam it. I was in a corner on the floor where he had beat me so bad. I crawled to the bathroom sink with tears rushing from my eyes with pain in my face and head. I pulled myself up and looked in the mirror I was shocked at what I saw. My nose was crocked and flat. My head had a big knot that was protruding from my scalp. My face was bruised. I didn't look like myself. I didn't want anyone to see me that way. Both of my eyes were blacked. My nose was bruised and swollen. I could hardly breathe out my nose. My nose bled inside my mouth all night long down my throat. I knew I needed to go to the doctor but I was too ashamed and how would I explained my injury. When he saw my face, he didn't seem to be bothered. It did not faze him of what he did to me. My face was so severely bruised I didn't want anyone to see me. I stayed in the house. I usually would walk down to the mailbox in our apartment complex to see if there was mail, but I was so ashamed. I would wait until night so no one could see me. I didn't want my neighbor to see me I did not tell anyone not even my mom. I would cry and wonder what I did so wrong to have this happen to me .my eating disorder still was there the more I got upset, the more I would throw up. My god, please help me make my life better take me far away, so peace will be in my life god please help me. After about 10 days my bruise on my face healed. The black eye and the swelling in my face and head had disappeared, so I made an appointment with the doctor about my nose since it was still crooked and flat. I went to the doctor to get x-rays of my nose and found out it was broken. The bone under my eye was broken. The doctor said I had to see a specialist because it was so damaged. He made an appointment with another doctor. When I returned home to tell that monster what the doctor said he acted like he didn't care. My nose and bone under my eye was broken. He didn't say anything. He did not care what our daughter saw him do to me.

My binging and purging was still with me. I ate as much food as I could in secret and went to the bathroom, locked the door, and threw it all up. I had a habit that I could not get rid of, but after throwing up, I felt a lot better even with a broken nose. I was still surviving. I finally went to the specialist about my nose. They did an x-ray of my nose and found out that my nose was broken in so many places that surgery would be needed. I was scheduled for surgery the next week. I never told anyone not even my family.

The time came for me to have surgery on my nose. I was so happy I hated the way my nose looked. it was so-so crooked. all I could remember is what he had told me over, and over that I'm going to break your nose right in the middle. It's like his plans had come true. I had a broken nose and outpatient surgery was needed.

I got all signed in. My daughter was with her dad. When it got closer to my surgery they gave me anesthesia to put me to sleep for the operation. I remember when they gave me that shot it felt like coolness going through my body. I said WOW! The doctor said the surgery would be three hours. I was shocked my nose must have been in bad shape to take so long. My entire nose had to be re-broken to put in back together again. I remember me laughing from the anesthesia. I couldn't stop. My daughter looked at me with a stare wondering what was wrong with me. I kept laughing even the nurse asked what was wrong with me. She should have known I just got a shot of pain medication, which made me laugh. Finally, I started getting quieter and started dozing off. My daughter kept her eyes on me. She just looked kind of sad to see her mom in the hospital bed. Her dad acted like nothing ever happen. He didn't appear to care he said it was all my fault that he hit me and I should have obeyed him and do what he asked me to do , and it would not have happened. He said the next time do what he said. It was not a big deal to him that I was in a hospital with a broken nose. I was just about sleep. I can remember them pushing my bed down the hallway to the operating room. I did not want my daughter to see me in the hospital but I didn't have anywhere else for her to stay. I did not have any family members. While I was on the operating table there was one more thing I could remember before I was out, someone lifting me out my bed to the operating bed. It was like they put my neck under something like a block. I was sleep after that. All I remember is waking up to someone calling my name. I finally woke up. The nurse asks me was I in some kind of car wreck. She also said I was very pretty. When my daughter saw me, she had this look in her eye. Why is my mom nose all bandaged and why is she wheeled down the hallway in a wheelchair. I love her so much I wanted to get out of this kind of life, but I honestly thought I was too stupid to make it on my own. It was time for me to go home. The nurse pushed me to the car. My nose felt funny but I was thankful it was repaired. When I returned home, I was hoping he would change and be sorry for what he has done and what I had to go through with my nose, but it was like he felt he didn't cause it. That made me so sad to know I had a severe breakage to my nose and the one who created it didn't seem to care. thanks be to God he was with me to carry me through. I could not wait to get healed and get back to my usual self. It took several weeks for my nose to heal. As the days went by I was rapidly improving.

As time went by my husband wanted to change his job position.. The only way he could change jobs was to cross train into another field . He put the paperwork in for telecommunications and good he was accepted. So we had to move away from Arizona to Texas so he could get trained on his new assignment. His new station was in Wichita Falls, Texas. His training would last one year, and after his training, we would be stationed somewhere else. As time got closer to moving, I was excited to leave Arizona. We had been there for five years. On the day of our departure, the mover came and packed up everything. I was happy that we didn't have to pack our things ourselves. The military was required to move you when you go to another station. After everything was packed and loaded on the truck the next day we traveled to Texas. I was excited to move and was glad because I wanted to put all bad memories behind me. I prayed to God that things will be different in our new home. Finally, we got there. It was the month of July and it was scorching hot in Texas. I was glad we moved in the summer months because of the warm travel conditions. We didn't have to worry about traveling while it was cold. We found a two bedroom apartment. My daughter was excited about Wichita Falls. There were lots of kids that she could play with. I would let her go outside to play with our neighbor's kid. I always watched her and kept my eye on her. I didn't trust anyone. I never left her unattended. She was so happy playing outside. I was happy that we had left Arizona hoping my prayer would be answered. No more abuse and no more pain. God I ask you to rescue me.

My daughter was 5 years old now and time for her to go to kindergarten. I was a little nervous about her going to school. On her first day of school we arrived at her room. all the kids were sitting at the table. She was so shy. I could tell she didn't want to be there and I didn't want to leave her. I asked her would you like to sit with the other kids at the table, she said not one word. I knew I had to leave. I could tell she wanted to cry, but she was strong. As I was leaving her with tears in my eyes, I kissed her and said I would be back in a few hours. I hope you have a great day. She looked so sad, but I left slowly out the door. We looked at each other until I was out the doorway. As I left, I cried all the way home. I felt so sorry to leave her. I was hoping and praying she would be ok, but I know God will protect her and comfort her. It was 3:00 and time to pick my girl up from school. I couldn't wait to ask her how her day had gone. I parked my car and went inside the school to wait by the door to meet her. I heard the bell ring and school were out. As I saw her coming out the door, I had such a great big smile on my face. I was so glad to see her, she had a huge smile that greeted me. I hugged her and asked her did she have a great day. She said it was a good day. I felt so much better. As time went on, I felt immensely happier.

I would dress her pretty with ruffle socks,sandals,and hair bows. one day her teacher ask me did I know my daughter could run fast she told me she would race the older boys to the fence during recess so I decided to go there and watch her run during her play time outside. Boy she could run really fast. she raced the older boys to the fence and dusted them. I was shocked to see how fast my daughter could run. the older boys she race was not happy that a kindergarten beat them .

Maybe the change of location softened my husband towards me. I was surprised he was not abusing me or making me feel bad about myself. I felt like God was fixing my marriage. We were there The year went by swiftly and before you know it he only had 6 more weeks of training. He received a package telling him he would be assigned to Nebraska. Wow, I thought that was a cold place. As we got down to the last week, it was time to move again.

When it came time for the move the packers came to assist us as they did before. As we moved out our apartment, we told our neighbors' goodbye. We had planned to go home for a few days before going to Nebraska. So we drove our car from Texas to our hometown. It was a long drive, but we finally made it there. I was happy to see my family. I was hoping things would be better than the last visit. I was glad to see my grandma. We stayed with my mother again. I didn't understand she had three bedrooms and always would allow us to sleep in that one room that had a bed that thick plastic on the mattress. All three of us had to sleep in there. A very tiny room with all our luggage. No drawers to put our clothes. We had to leave our clothes in the suitcase. I didn't understand why we all had to sleep in that bed. I didn't say anything it was her house. I was just a visitor. I tried to make the best of it by ignoring my mother funny ways. She didn't want you cooking in her kitchen or sitting on her couch. She even had plastic on that. She was so particular about everything. I tried to stay away as much as possible from home. She was always looking to see if you had messed up anything. Such looking in the trash cans in the bedroom we slept in. It was almost time to leave to go to Omaha, Nebraska. One evening, he began to fuss at me over nothing. the more I told him I didn't want to hear it the more he became angry. He started calling me names you stupid, you idiot, dumb ass bitch. I told him to shut up. that's when he punched me and threw me down on the hardwood floor. I fell backward, and the back of my head hit the floor so hard I laid there in pain. I knew that the back of my head was bleeding. I was in so much pain. I was so scared to get up my head was pounding in pain. I was laying there listening to words coming from his mouth saying if you could have shut your mouth this would not have happened. You talk too damn much, idiot. As I raised my self-up off the floor standing to my feet, I stumble to the bathroom to look at myself in the mirror. I cried out to God. Lord, here it goes again. Save me Lord from this violence I'm in. My head wasn't bleeding, but I did have a big lump in the back of my head. As I came out the bathroom, I screamed at him why you keep hurting me over and over. He ran up to me and said because you won't shut your big ass mouth. I told him I could talk when I please and say whatever I like and I'm not shutting up anymore. He shoved me.

I hit the wall. My poor baby saw everything. I grabbed my daughter and left the house. I didn't care if he was left there without any car. I just went out driving with tears rolling down my face. I said to myself I better stop crying I didn't want my daughter to see me cry anymore so I stopped. We only had a few more days left to leave so I visited everyone to tell everyone goodbye. As the day came to leave we packed up everything and loaded the car. I said goodbye again and off we drove off to Nebraska. It was a 12-hour drive but it was not like the drive from Arizona. We finally made it to a very cold Nebraska. It was in the winter time. We stayed in the military hotel until we found an apartment. Our new apartment was a little small but we managed. One day while in the apartment we saw a mouse in there. We got a mouse trap and caught it. Once we caught it we threw it outside. The next day we saw another one. Wow, I said where all the mouse all coming from. Then I thought its cold outside they were looking for a warm place.

It was 1992. I was now 25 years old. We finally found an apartment we stayed in the military hotel for 3 weeks. We finally moved out into a two bedroom apartment. It was very big compared to that small studio apartment we lived in Arizona. I was so happy to live in our own apartment. our furniture arrived from the movers. We unpacked all our things. It was time for us to find our daughter a school. She had been out for a while now. She still in kindergarten. It was a school down the street so we enrolled her in it.

They had morning session or afternoon sessions for kindergarten. I chose afternoon because I didn't want to get up so early. I was surprised she wasn't shy as she was before. I was so happy about that. My husband was getting himself signed in to the base we were at. He had lots of paperwork to take care of. Usually, I would take him to work and take my daughter to school. One day it was so cold outside way below zero. My husband had to use the car that day so he took our daughter to school. On his lunch break, he came home and said he would pick her up at 3:00 that's when school was out. I was ok with that but as it got closer to that time, I began to watch the clock. It was now 3:10 and no sign of him returning home with her. The school was just down the hill from our apartment maybe half a mile. I started to get worried. I put on some clothes and started walking down the icy sidewalk to school to find out she had not been picked up. I didn't have a hat on my head or ears covered up. It was way below zero degrees as I got closer to the school I could see my daughter standing on the side of the streets waiting for someone to pick her up. I tried to walk faster and even run but I couldn't go fast because of the icy sidewalk. Cars were passing me the passengers in the cars was looking like what is wrong with this woman walking on this very cold day with below zero temperature. I didn't care I just wanted my daughter. As I walked I saw a man grabbed her hand and took her away. I screamed her name but I was not close enough so she could hear me. I began to panic. I wanted to take her home. I walked as fast as I could with tears running down my face. Oh God protect her and save her from whatever the enemy has planned for her. Finally, she had walked out of my sight. It was a terrible thing to see your little girl guided away with a stranger and you can't help her. Finally, her dad came down the street it was 3:40 school was out at 3:00. He saw me walking and blew the horn. I ran and got in the car. Finally, we arrived at the school. I open the door and ran out of the car and hurried to the school. there I found my daughter sitting in a chair unharmed. I cried and cried and grabbed her. I was so thankful she was safe. The man who rescued her was a janitor of the school he told me he didn't want her standing outside by herself so he brought her back in the school. I thanked him. It could have been the opposite. But God loved her and kept his arms all around her. As we left the school and got back in the car. I sat in the backseat. I let her sit in the front. I was so shaken up. I noticed my ear was hurting really bad it was swelling. I didn't know what was wrong with it as we were driving home. My little girl kept looking back at me in the car. Finally, she reached in her pocket a pulled out something she made at school and said mommy this is for you that I made. I cried and smiled and said thank you. I loved you so much. She turned her head and looked straight ahead. My ear continue to hurt. I could not wait to get home and look at my ear. It felt very hard. Finally, we made it home. I went inside our apartment when I looked in the mirror I said oh my god. My ear was so big and was turning black it was hard to touch. I decided to go to the emergency room. The doctor told me that my ear was frostbitten from having my ears uncovered. I wasn't outside that long. I guess the temperature was so cold, but I wanted my daughter to be safe. If I had to do it over, I would have walked outside in the cold weather just for her. The doctor said that I might have a problem with that ear for the rest of my life. When we left the hospital on our way home. I felt so sad knowing that my five-year-old daughter was by herself on the side of the street in Nebraska, it was a big city. She could have been abducted. When we arrived home, I asked him why he was so late picking her up. He said he just lost track of time. I told him that was important he should have been more responsible. That made him so mad he did not want me telling him anything. So he said shut up that why your ear is the way it is for walking your stupid ass outside into the cold uncovered. I told him it was stupid to forget her he got angry and slapped me across my face and punch me in the stomach . it took the air out of me I could not breath . that was a horrible feeling. I was rolling around on the floor he said shut the hell up bitch always running your damn mouth. I said that my daughter that could have been hurt. He said you say something else this time I bet you will shut up. I didn't say anything else so I did not have to fight everything I do or say is never right.   I wanted a better life, a better husband. It has been 6 years now, and nothing has changed my life is still tortured with so much pain so much hurt will it ever change.

Nebraska was a place with cold winters. We had blizzards every week. Nebraska was not a place where I would want to stay the rest of my life. When we left from Arizona, we were hoping our next assignment would be Florida, but we ended up in Nebraska. I have to make the best of it while we are there we had an apartment until base housing was available.

I couldn't wait till we had our name on the list for the military housing. We stayed in that apartment for about 6 months. Finally we got a call that they had a two-bedroom house for us. I was so excited to be moving on the base. We lived where all military family was together. That should be fun I thought as we settle into our new house. We enrolled her in a school right outside the base. She seemed like she was excited about her new school. I met some friends on the base that I talked to sometimes. I always made sure that my daughter had breakfast before she went to school. I kept her nice and clean every day. She was a very good girl she never was disobedient. She always was respectful. One day we went to an amusement park called Penny Park. That is the one time in my life that was special. Her dad was nice that day he carried our daughter on his shoulders.

I didn't know Nebraska had thunderstorms. I thought they only had winter storms. One day the weatherman predicted severe weather. My neighbors were preparing for stormy weather. We just didn't pay any attention to the weather. That night the weather started getting bad. Very stormy outside the tornado sirens went off. We had a basement outside of the house and we didn't go down in the basement. Everybody else did but we stayed in our house. Finally, we had a knock at the door. One of our neighbors told us we should come to the shelter that it would be safer. So we left out of our house. It was raining and the wind was blowing so hard. I didn't understand why my husband was running without us. He was in front. I was holding our daughter. she was scared but I held her tight. He left us behind that made me feel terrible. it's like we didn't matter, if we made it to the basement or not. we did and all of our neighbors were there. He looked so stupid that someone had to come and get us out of our house. Spring was approaching and warm weather was starting to come. The school semester was almost over. My little girl would be out for the summer.

We wanted a new car so we went car hunting and found a pretty red Hyundai Coupe. It was a brand new car and I was so excited. We drove our new car home. We had two cars now. I was so happy with the new car. one day as I was driving down the highway I had to stop at a stop sign. I heard this loud noise. a big SUV truck had hit me from the back and pushed into the SUV truck in from of me. my daughter were in the car with me. it jerked my neck so hard. I looked over and asked my little girl was she ok. And she said she was. I got out the car to found out that my car was so badly damaged in the back and front. The hood was sticking up. It looked really bad, but I could drive it home. My husband was surprised to see that I was in an accident and the way the car looked. I was so thankful that my daughter was ok and not hurt from the accident. when my husband found out about the wreck he called me all kinds of names you so stupid and dumb you cannot drive and that I needed to go to a class for dummies and get some driving skills. he said I should have known you can't drive but it was not my fault and he knew it. I was sitting still at a red light and a SUV pushed me into another SUV.

He just wanted to make me feel bad about myself.

Our little red car had to go to the repair body shop. It took a month for repair because of some of the parts. During that time we had a rental vehicle, so that helped out a lot. After a month passed we finally got our car back. I was so happy to be driving that pretty red car again. You could not even tell that it had been damaged. What a happy day that was. It was now going into the fall in Nebraska and one day he came home from work and said he was going to hang with some of the guys that night. I just had a very funny feeling about that. He left about 7:00 that night. I hated that I and my daughter was left alone. It was now 9:00 and I thought he would have been home by now. 10:00 o'clock passed he still wasn't back then 11:00 passed and he still wasn't at home. Around about 11:15 I found a telephone number where he was going. I was shocked a woman answered the phone. I hung up when I heard her voice. I just had a funny feeling he was going to a woman house. I was so upset. 12:00 he finally came home. I asked him why was he gone so late and why did he tell me he was going over some guy's house from the base. I told him I found a number of the house you were going to and a lady answered. He got so mad at me he started yelling at me calling me names you so stupid you crazy bitch. I yelled back and told him not to call me that name again. He got angry as I talked back to him he started to approach me and got close in my face and swung me into the wall. My body had busted the wall he shoved me so hard. I fell to the floor. I could not get off the floor. I cried with tears down my face. My arms, back and legs hurt, then he left. He didn't care how bad I was hurt or even help me up. I was left alone that night lonely worried about where he had gone. Depressed and sorrowful all I asked him why a woman answered that number that supposed to have been a guy house. He knew I had caught him in a lie so he made me pay for confronting him in his lie. My body had bruised from that push into the wall. My body had broken the wall so badly that it looks like the print of my body. He never came to help me. He never asked if I was ok. he never cared if I was hurt. He went to sleep as if nothing happen. I could barely get in the bed. I was so sore with bruises on my body. I cried myself to sleep very quietly so no one could hear me. I prayed to god to save me, Lord. This pain inside this abuse that in my life just won't seem to go away.. That next morning my husband acted as nothing happen. I could barely get up out the bed and walk down the stairs. He never cared to find out how I felt or even care about the big hole in the wall. He left and went to work he didn't even say goodbye. I walked slowly around the house my body was so sore from being thrown into a wall. My daughter was sleep that night when that happens. I was so glad she didn't see or hear what had gone on that night. When my husband returned home from work that evening, I showed him the wall and what he had did to me. He said keep your stupid mouth shut up and you wouldn't have gotten pushed. He said that what's happen when you keep running your big ass mouth. I felt like nothing inside. I felt like why I'm even living, my life haven't gotten any better. We never sat down and discussed the problems because everything that happens was my fault. He never would admit to anything he did wrong. I finally healed from all those bruises on me, but the wall wasn't fixed. Every time I passed by that wall, it reminded me of being thrown into it. I closed my eyes every time I passed that way. he was so mean and cruel to me. I told no one. I kept it a secret. I was so ashamed of what happened. To this day I wonder if our neighbor heard all of that racket. When I would pass them outside, I would look the other way so I could not make eye contact. I know it was such a bad thing that happened.

We have been in Nebraska for a year and eight months. We wanted so bad to be assigned to Florida. If he took an overseas assignment upon our return he would have the base of his choice. So he put in for assignment overseas. It didn't take long. He came home with news that he had assignment overseas to Izmir, Turkey. We had 60 days before leaving. Before we left I went back to a clothing store that I went to in Nebraska just to look around. It was a guy that works there he had eyes that went up like a cat, and he wore glasses. I used to see him working in the store he would always look at me. He never would say anything he was a very dark man. When he saw me those eyes I never will forget them. He reaches into his pocket and reach out his hand and to greet me When I left I notice it was a powerful cologne scent on my hand. I could not wait to get home to wash my hands I washed and washed my hands the smell would not leave. I was thinking what kind of cologne is this. It almost like it had to wear out I started thinking maybe he was into witchcraft and tried to put a spell on me. I didn't go back to that store again.

We had planned to go home and visit our parents before went on our two-year assignment. We had a lot to do. We had to get passports and shots. We had to get packed. . The military gave us brochures about the country of Turkey and their culture. I listen very closely to the briefing on Turkey. Their country had schools for American children, but it was not with the Turkish children. It was only for American that was in the military. They didn't have base housing, so we have to stay in the Turkish apartments with the Turkish living there. I thought it would be different.

It was time for our household good to get packed. We were now leaving Nebraska. We had two cars we were going to take one car with us and leave the other one in storage. On the day we left I drove the pretty red car, and he drove the other one. I had to trail him back to our hometown. It was a 12-hour drive. My daughter rode with me. As we drove down the interstate, I followed close behind him because I didn't know the way back. It was a very busy interstate, but I did great as I followed behind him. He decided to switch over I switched also, but then he switched again so fast I couldn't move over because a car was behind me the lane I was in took me off the interstate. He had kept going. We were separated. I just pulled over on the shoulder and stopped. I was hoping he would turn around and find us. We waited and waited, and it was 2 hours had passed. It was getting dark. I began to get nervous and worried I didn't know where I was at and how to get home I remember the man in the store of the handshaking did he put a hex on me and cause these bad things. Everything was going through my mind. When I turned my focus to god and said a silent prayer I felt better. I didn't want my baby girl to know how scared I was. I started to leave and try to find my way back but I heard a voice say stay your help is on the way. Finally, as I open up my eyes I saw a white car coming up it was my husband. He found us. He may not come when you want him but he is always on time. I asked why you were driving so fast. I couldn't move over so quickly cars were coming so fast behind me. He knew we were scared and frightened. So we drove off down the interstate once again as we drove for about 3 hours I noticed the car I was driving started sounding funny and it would not pull or go as fast. I signaled for him to pulled over to see what was wrong. He said the transmission of the red car was going out. So we had to find a hotel in that town because it was late. We had to wait until the next morning so we could take the car to the shop. We took everything out the car and put it in the white car. And waited until the car dealership opens up the next morning.

We left the car I can't remember what town we were in. The mechanic said the transmission was gone out that car was practically new. We had not had it that long it was still under warranty. So we left it and would come back and pick it up when they finish. I was so thankful I didn't keep driving. God knew that if I had kept driving I would have been along on the interstate just me and my little girl with the transmission gone out but God keeps me from what the devil planned for me. Thank you, Jesus, as we drove another 100 hundred miles we noticed that the second car we were in had a knocking in the engine. I couldn't believe what was happening the engine had gone out.. It seemed like we could never get to our hometown. We had to stay another two nights. we checked into a hotel again . that car didn't have any warranty. So we rented a U-Haul truck and towed the white car back to our hometown. I just could not believe that both cars had problems, The new car transmission was gone out and the white car the motor was gone out. We spent an extra 4 days total on the highway. It's like we couldn't get back home. it was so strange to me.

Finally we made it home. We had 30 days to be in our hometown before we left for Turkey. I was glad to be back home again even if I wasn't close with my family. We stayed with my mother again. She didn't act like she was that excited to see us. Maybe because she knew we were going to be staying with her those weeks before we left. I was surprised she let us stay there. It was December when we were there .I remember being so cold in my mother house. My daughter and I both caught a cold there It was so cold in her house She hardly ever put the heater on. Our time there wasn't the best, but I tried to make the best of it. My mom had her same ways. Still wouldn't let us have a bed to our self. we had to sleep in that full-size bed, all three of us. Her granddaughter was 7 years old. we had a month to be in that house and it was so uncomfortable. I remember asking her could I cook in her kitchen. She was very particular it was like she only wanted us to just stay in that small bedroom because she thought we would mess up and dirty her house. I wish I had a mother that was loving. As time went by we had another week in a half before we left the United States to go to Turkey. My oldest sister and her husband were trying to discourage me from going. they said they didn't have houses or apartments over there, and we would have to live in huts. I explained to them that where we were going had apartments, but they didn't believe me. I also said the military would not allow the family to be station over there if they had huts. They were very negative about it. Time had passed by it was time to leave. I told my family goodbye I was very nervous about living overseas. On our way to the airport, I was sad to leave. I was trying to appear that I was happy as we aboard the plane we flew all the way Washington DC and from DC we went to JFK airport in New York. It was so huge with very big planes. It was an international airport we got all our belonging checked in so we sat to wait until it was time to board our plane. As I looked out the window at some of the big planes they were so huge. I had never seen planes that big before. My daughter was amazed to see the airplanes. She had her little doll with her. I try to make sure she held on to it so I tried to keep an eye on it so she wouldn't lose it. We were delayed in the airport because our plane had mechanical issues. So we had to wait another 2 hours. It was a long wait so we got on another plane. We finally boarded the big huge plane. It had upstairs. I guess it had to be that large to go so far distant. As we took off on our ride to Izmir, Turkey we kept getting higher in the air. The plane had two levels and lots of TVs to watch it was very cold on that plane. we kept our coats on the entire time. It was about a 16-hour ride. My daughter didn't seem scared she enjoyed her ride. Finally, we enter in Turkey airport. it was so different over there. the people looked different from Americans. I was very nervous after checking through customs and getting our luggage. Outside there were yellow taxi cab everywhere. We didn't have a problem getting one. They also had horse carriage outside of the airport. Turkey was different there building and everything looked totally different. He got us a cab we put our things in and we told the cab driver where we wanted to go which was the Kordon Hotel. That where we would be staying until we get our apartment. There were lots of Americans that was already there. The Kordon was a tall historical looking apartment. It was not very pretty it had lots of floors. Our room was not pretty either but there nothing I could do but get used to it. The water smelled bad when you cut on the faucet. Sometimes I would see big roaches as long as your finger that really scared me and my daughter. I would call her dad when we saw these ugly roaches. I have never seen a roach that big in my life. We would keep the bathroom door closed because it was a smell that came out the drains that were very unpleasant, they had a restaurant that was inside the apartment.This is where we ate breakfast, lunch, and dinner. The food wasn't that bad. It was kind of nice. We met some other military families while in the hotel apartment. One family we met had a little girl almost the same age as my daughter. They seemed nice.

The next day we went to find an apartment and my husband was going to check himself into the base. We got into a taxi and the Turkish cab driver pulled out a bundle of American money and asked us if would we get him some supplies from the Base Exchange. He said he could get us some Turkish rugs very cheap if we would do that favor for him. he had a list with all kind of stuff to get. My husband said he would go and get them for him. He thought that he could get some Turkish stuff without paying their prices. the briefing we had before we left came back to my mind. the guy told us not to buy any American goods for the Turkish people. he warned us what would happen If caught we would get to that bad terrible prison. I reminded him of what we were told before we left. he said let just do it this time and we won't do it again. I had a very bad feeling something just didn't feel right but he had taken the guy money anyway. I could not rest that night. I told him to give it back to him. I believed it was a set up to destroy our life. The next morning he went and found that taxi driver and told him we were not going to be able to purchase those items for him and walked off.

We finally did get to look for a place to live. We didn't want apartments with the Turkish style toilet. The Turkish toilet was just a hole in the floor with a string that you pull to flush it. there is no way I could get used to that but finally, we found an apartment that looked pretty nice. It was going to take a couple of weeks before our furniture would arrive but in the meantime, we stayed at Kordon Hotel.

Turkey was so different from the United States. I would always dream of the day to return to the United States. We met a lot of military families while we were there. There was not a lot of jobs to apply for only the American jobs. I decided to apply for some of the jobs that were open. I applied for a job at the base exchange which was like a department store. I was so excited when I got an interview and was hired for the position. I was hired to answer the telephone at the Base Exchange. my husband continued to mistreat me and call me ugly names. I wish I could have better my life with an education so I could take care of myself and my daughter. what was so bad about me I just didn't understand why. While working at the BX one day a military guy came in the store. He asked me a question. I can't remember his question. He told me that I look sad all the time. I never would tell him why I was sad or what was going on in my life. He would always come in and say nice kind things to me. It just made me feel special. I would love if my husband could say kind things to me. As he kept coming inside the store he would always stop and say something nice. it was pleasant to hear nice things for once. I would come home wishing that my husband would be nice to me. I felt so alone. When the guy came in he would always ask me how my day was. One day he asked me when my birthday was. I told him and he didn't forget, he gave me some earrings. I couldn't accept those items because I felt guilty. I told him that I was married .but it was a good feeling that someone wanted to do something nice for me. That put a smile on my face. I would think why I have to be called horrible names and disrespected and put down, physically and mentally abused by the man I married. I always stayed sad but if I

could only get out and had the strength. I would think to myself
I wanted my husband to talk to me nice like the guy in the store. I
wish my husband could have been different toward me.   I told my
husband that this guy ask me when was my birthday and offer to give
me some earrings but I didn't accept them. I told him he would
come to the store to talk to me. I told him I was married. my
husband got upset with me. since he working in
telecommunications he had the advantage to spy on me or even tap
the phone line. He thought maybe I was talking on the phone at
work or something. One day I went to work. He decided to listen in
on a call that was received. he thought he would hear me talking to
someone but he didn't hear me talking. he told his other coworker s
what he had done. When I came home from work he began to
question me about the guy who would come into the store and
bother me.   He said he believes it was more to it. I told him it was
nice to hear someone talk nice. I told him all I hear is bad negative
things. I wish I was with someone else who really appreciated me.

I want a husband that was respectful and truly   love me. that
night he ask me a question about the guy. I had told him that he
was just saying nice things to me. he ask me questions over and over
again .I could not get any sleep all night long he kept going over the
same thing over and over again. it was about four in the morning
and he would not let me get any sleep.   I didn't have anything to tell
him only that the guy would come into the store and he asks me
when was my birthday and he offered to give me some earrings. He

said maybe that would put a smile on my face. He said he was just giving it to me because he thought I was a nice person. I didn't accept them because I loved my husband. I was so tired. all night long he questioned me. I had nothing to tell him. I never went back to that job again. I was telling him the truth. I remember as I was walking out of the room to go to sleep. He grabbed me by my arm and then he grabs a can of starch from off of the table that you use for clothes. He tried to spray it on my face and my daughter woke up and ran into the room. She was yelling!!!!!!!!! Mommy close your eyes he was trying to put my eyes out. I closed my eyes so the starch would not get into my eyes. My daughter tried to pull him away from me. She begs him to put that can down. all she ever saw was her dad fighting her mom. Then all of a suddenly he told our daughter you know I only married your mother because of you. She said don't you love mom. I said I am so tired of you being a monster in front of our daughter. We don't deserve to live this kind of life. I ask him why you would tell a little girl something like that. Then he took his hand and punch me on the side of my face and ear. He hit me so fast I did not see it coming. Immediately I couldn't hear out the right ear. it was like it had water in it or I was on an airplane. he didn't even care. I told him about my ear he just walked away like nothing happen. I grabbed my ear I kept saying my ear. it was throbbing with pain it was so sore to touch. After a week went by my ear didn't get any better. I made an appointment to go to the doctor. when I got to the doctor, they did x-rays on my ear and found out that I had a busted eardrum. I was shocked. wow I said. the doctor asked me how did it happen. I made up a story that I was playing basketball and the ball hit me in the ear. the doctor said that I was going to have to see a specialist in Ramstein Germany to see If I need surgery. he set me up an appointment.I had to fly up there on a military plane. I was so nervous because I had to go by myself I did not want to leave my daughter I did not want to go but I didn't have a choice. I had to leave on the military bus that would picked me up in front of the Kordon hotel. it was so hard to say goodbye to my little girl. she didn't know that I was going to the doctor about my ear.   I told her that I had to take care of something.   she didn't want to stay there with her dad because she knew he was mean without me and all the bad things he had done to me. I felt she didn't deserve to have a life seeing her mother get beat up all the time. I really do love my daughter she was the best thing that could have happened to me.   I was gone a week. I wish my daughter could have been there with me. I can't remember why they didn't go.

I didn't want to travel in a foreign country by myself. It was scary riding through Turkey on the bus seeing all the different towns and Turkish people. When I got to the military plane other military people were on the plane as well going to Germany to visit the doctor. I was thinking I wanted a better life for my daughter and I, while riding on the plane.

When I got to Germany, I stayed in a hotel on the base in Ramstein.   I met this girl in the hotel. She told me about things that happened in her life she was abused as a child. She would steal. She said she was a terrible person but God saved her and filled her with the Holy Spirit with the evidence of speaking in tongues. I didn't know what she was talking about I never heard of that before but I kept on listening to her talk. She said she had the gift of interpretation of hearing what other people say when they speak in tongues. I said to myself she seems like a very nice person but I never forgot what she told me. I used to think about her all the time I thought it was strange, the conversation we had it was something so different about her.

The next day I saw the doctor, he told me that I would not have to have surgery. He believed it would heal up on its own. He told me do not wash my hair for about three weeks because of the hole in my eardrum. If I did I would lose my hearing. I thank God he gave me the knowledge to go to the doctor. I really missed my daughter. I would call back to our house. I was so glad to talk to her I told her I would be home the next day. The doctor told me that I may always have problems with that ear. hen I arrived back to Izmir, Turkey I was glad to be united with my daughter again. As time went by my ear healed.

I didn't understand why my husband told his coworkers that he was listening to the conversation at a government facility while his wife was at work. His co-workers reported to their boss about what he told them and they investigated the situation. They found out it was true and they charged him with wire taping at a government facility. They made a big thing out of it and the military file a complaint on him. It was a nightmare. I was questioned about what he did. They removed him from his telecommunication job to another job until the investigation was over. I was so afraid. I was questioned over and over and over again. I didn't know anything about it. They wanted to prosecute him. I was followed everywhere I went even when I sat down to have lunch. There was a guy sat close to listen to my conversation. When I met one of my friends at the Base Exchange to have lunch. I notice this same guy was always close by everywhere. God revealed to me what he was doing. They wanted to hear me say something about what they suspected my husband did. I didn't know anything about what he had done. It was a nightmare. I was scared to go out because I thought I was being followed for what my husband had did. I did not know about what was happening. It went on for 2 years. I didn't want him to go to jail. It was like the devil had plans for him from the time he stepped into Turkey. It started with the cab driver wanted him to go and buy American goods and he almost fell into that trap. I didn't want him to go to prison for taping a phone. Why would he do something so insane and then tell his co-workers. The guys that follow me was listening to see if I was talking to someone about what they were accused of doing. I was so stressed out and worried every day. I was so scared to come out of our apartment. The more I was stressed the more I threw up. I could not get that eating disorder out of my life. No one knew what was going on in my life when I threw up. it was a release. I wanted it to go away but I could not help myself. the more stress and worried I was the worst it got. I had my eating disorder about 7 or 8 years now and I kept it a secret. I was very thin everybody thought I was just dieting.

I met some Christian friends who kept me uplifted and prayed for us. I now realize God had to take me through something to get my attention. He took me to Turkey so I would not ever be the same again. Everything that happens was for a reason. As time went by we got involved in the church and were encouraged by our Christian friends. They taught us about the bible and what God is able to do that is one time my husband was not so mean to me.

Finally, the trial started. We were all in the courtroom. I still remember that morning of the trial, the judge said everyone rise all of my Christian friends attended I never told my daughter what was going on. I didn't want her to know.

As I sat in the courtroom on the front row with tears in my eyes scared to death. I had learned a lot about God now with the help of my friends, they really were there for us. I thank God for each and every one of them if he would have been found guilty he would have gone to prison for so many years. The trial went on for four days. There was a plane each day of the trial. He was required to pack his clothes daily in case he was found guilty.

They had a plane outside waiting to take him to prison. I was so scared. I was thinking what I would do if he leaves and goes to prison. I was in a foreign country many thousands of miles from the United States. I had a 7-year-old daughter. What if they find him guilty him I thought, but God knows best? As the trial began I listen to all the different people talk on the witness stand. That was one time he was not cruel at the time he was in trouble. I sat there almost about to faint. I got up and went to the bathroom and kneel down before God and said dear Jesus come in this courtroom and take completely over. I said either I am going to trust God or give up. the devil spoke in my ear and said if he is convicted go home and take a bottle of pills and die. I got so weak. I wanted to die if he went to prison. I had taken all I could take I was going to kill myself.

As I left the bathroom, God said to come back and pray one more time. I said, Jesus, I need you to forgive me. I am sorry. Please don't take my husband. I'm all alone. Set him free so I and my daughter won't be in this country alone. I opened the door and walked out to my seat when the jury returned with their verdict. They found him not guilty. I was so happy they said he could never work in telecommunications again. He lost his military clearance. My two-year nightmare was over.

It was time to return to the United States in January 1995. My husband decided to take an early retirement after ten years of serving in the military air force. I really did like the military. I didn't want him to get out but I guess all the trouble that had gone on that season of my life was over. I truly thank god for all the friends I met while in Turkey that helps me through those tough fiery trials. They taught me the word of God and what he can do they were truly a blessing in my life. They will always be a part of my memories .when we return to the U.S the airplane ride back was very long.

We arrived in Macon Georgia at a military base we stayed about three days. That is where he was discharged from the military. We stayed at the base hotel. My husband told me again he only married me because of my daughter. He said he wanted somebody with a degree and I was not good enough for him. I would never be up to his level or ever make more money than him because I was too stupid and dumb. I said this man was only being somewhat nice to me because he wanted God to get him out of trouble. He still was the same person. He went back to his old self. I told him he knew I did not have a degree when he married me. I was not a lazy person and I tried to do the best I could but nothing was never good enough for him.

After he finishes his discharge process we flew back to our hometown. I was so tired of hearing all of his abuse. I wanted to be free I did not want to have a life living in fear anymore I did not want my daughter to be raised in a dysfunctional home. I wanted to get out. I was tired now. I wanted to be free. I depended on him for everything and he knew I could not take care of myself. He had all the money and the control. I was helpless. My mom knew I was coming back home after being gone for two years. I called my mom to come and get us she said something was wrong with her car. So we had to call another family member in my husband family to come and get us. It was a very old dirty van with curtain swinging back and forth. I was sad my mother could not pick us up. I really did miss her. My husband relative took us to my mother house. When I got to her house I found out nothing was wrong with her car she just didn't want to pick us up. I thought she would have been glad to see me since I was gone for two years. I needed to make a decision about my life. I did not want to go through any more abuse. All my memories were bad I had no good ones. I did not know if I should stay married to him. I wanted my daughter to have a better life. I knew I needed to leave. I was so afraid to take that first step. I knew I had a decision to make for me and my daughter. It was time for us to be happy and have a life that was not being abused. I saw on a television advertisement of victims that have been abused and battered. I wrote down the number and the address so I and my daughter could be happy. I wanted to be free from abuse and having an eating disorder. I wanted a life I never had but only I and the strength of God can get me out. I am going to call them now let see what happens.............

FINAL THOUGHT

Before the publishing of *Life after the Storm*, my uncle passed away. He never talked about the things that he did or asked us for forgiveness. We forgave him. I pray that he asked God to forgive him.

ABOUT THE AUTHOR

Janice is a native of Tennessee but now lives in Arkansas. She has a
lovely daughter and a wonderful husband. Janice loves God and
gives inspirational and motivational messages to anyone she comes in
contact with. *Life after the Storm* is her first published work.

Made in the USA
Coppell, TX
11 September 2021